THE
KARMA
OF CATS

THE
KARMA
OF CATS

spiritual wisdom from our feline friends

AN ANTHOLOGY EDITED BY
DIANA VENTIMIGLIA

sounds true
BOULDER, COLORADO

Sounds True
Boulder, CO 80306

Published 2019

Book design by Beth Skelley

Printed in South Korea

Library of Congress Cataloging-in-Publication Data

Names: Ventimiglia, Diana, editor.
Title: The Karma of cats : spiritual wisdom from our feline friends / edited by Diana Ventimiglia.
Description: Boulder, CO : Sounds True, 2019.
Identifiers: LCCN 2019007814 (print) | LCCN 2019018431 (ebook) | ISBN 9781683643210 (ebook) |
  ISBN 9781683642534 (pbk.)
Subjects: LCSH: Cats—Religious aspects.
Classification: LCC BL443.C3 (ebook) | LCC BL443.C3 K37 2019 (print) | DDC 202/.12—dc23
LC record available at https://lccn.loc.gov/2019007814

10 9 8 7 6 5 4 3 2 1

Contents

ABOVE Seane and Zooey

Introduction

Seane Corn

Cats are everything to me. I cannot imagine a life in which cats don't dominate my world. Anyone who has ever had a cat burrow into their neck, heart, and consciousness knows that this relationship is way bigger than just being a cat's "owner" or "caretaker" or even their "parent." None of these roles quite defines the unique bond we have with these mysterious and wonderful creatures.

Our cats come to us. They find us. They show up in our little human worlds to teach us essential life lessons. And if we allow these lessons to permeate our awareness, they will change who we are, and we will be better for it.

I've often marveled at the cosmic dynamics between humans and felines, certain that cats are really our spirit guides or angels made manifest in these fluffy, furry, and complicated forms. Cats awaken us to our own human and spiritual potential, and this growth is accelerated through the compassion and care we lavish upon them.

In my experience, cats are at once incredibly loving, tender, and gentle—and also completely dismissive, rude, and indifferent. That's why we love them! We must learn to be present, responsive, aware, and unconditionally loving with these independent beings. There's no training or forcing them to do anything they don't want to do. They're probably not going to come when you call or sit on demand, and there's a good chance they'll pee in your favorite shoe—or maybe that's just me. But, my God, when a cat decides to show you love, it is a force field of sweetness like no other.

Cats are just the best. The worst. The best. If you're reading this and have relationships with cats in your own life, you probably understand exactly what I mean.

When I look at the trajectory of my life and the cats who have shown up for me, I have no doubt that there's been some sort of karmic bond behind our relationships. Cats have always come at just the right time, offering the perfect lessons to help me grow, learn, love, and even to let go.

In the yogic tradition, karma is the yoga of action, the law of cause and effect. By moving toward our karma with the intention to heal, we are able to transcend the ego and the limited beliefs it carries. Dealing with our karma, learning our essential lessons, is our path to fulfilling our purpose. And that purpose? To learn the power of spiritual love. To open our hearts to that love and then offer it back into the world in ways that are of benefit to all.

In order for us to do all this, though, we need guidance. We need teachers to reflect back the necessary wisdom that can lead to our growth. Sometimes their teachings are loving, and sometimes they are fierce. Always they will awaken our spirits and help our souls to mature.

Our teachers come in many forms, and I believe one of these forms is in the shape of a cat. Just when we need it most, the perfect kitty appears—at least perfect for us—to be our teacher and help us heal. That is the karma of cats: to lead us into our purpose by teaching us how to love unconditionally.

I have no doubt that the cats in my life have been significant karmic teachers—whether they taught me to play and be in my body, to develop my capacity for intimacy and trust, or to learn about death and loss. Ever since I was a little girl, there's been a cat in my life who has brought me right to the heart of my soul's next steps, opening me to greater capacities for love along the way. Thank God for them, for life could've been that much more scary to navigate without their wild and wondrous presence.

My first cats were Morris and Mittens. They lived for eighteen years and were with me for my entire childhood. They had a huge impact on my early life lessons.

Morris Twinkie Meow-Meow Corn was a big, orange tabby male—super alpha and the toughest dude on the block. After a couple of years in our life, Morris was hit by a car and lost an eye, but that didn't stop him from being the coolest cat ever. Despite being a one-eyed badass, Morris would exhibit the most unimaginable tenderness and babylike behavior. He used to lie on me and wean, kneading his paws back and forth on my neck, giving me little slurpy kisses, his purrs filled with drool and devotion. The way that Morris embodied these two extremes—tough and tender—made it okay for me to be in both my strength and vulnerability, too.

Our cats come to us. They find us. They show up in our little human worlds to teach us essential life lessons.

Mittens was a large, awkward, feisty girl who preferred to be alone, often indifferent and scornful to everyone other than me. Mittens wasn't an endearing cat. She'd be playing and loving one minute, then out of nowhere she'd latch onto your arm and scratch you repeatedly with her back paws. And yet we had this special relationship. She opened me to love the unlovable and to see the sweetness that sometimes others can't see, especially within myself.

My first kitty as a young adult was Tweetie, who came into my life when I was about nineteen, a couple of years after I moved to New York City. She was the most vicious, grumpy, and unpleasant animal you've ever known—but I thought she was spectacular. A feral New York street cat who would demand affection, then tolerate exactly two strokes before she would bite your hand and hiss, Tweetie always let you know that everything would be on her terms. She knew how to take care of herself. Tweetie showed me what resiliency and independence were, which would also prove to be the very qualities I needed in order to navigate New York on my own.

And then there were Billy and Butch—adorable, childlike, and very needy brothers who'd been weaned and taken away from their mother too soon. They taught me how to play, be spontaneous, and, most important, how to be a mother—to them and to myself.

There was also the very sensual and beautiful Daisy—one of my great loves. She was a nightmare. She adored men, was very flirty, and demanded attention. If she didn't get it to her satisfaction, she would literally climb on your chest while you were sleeping and pee on you. She taught me about self-confidence, about how to speak up and ask for my needs to be met. Most importantly, she taught me how to forgive.

And my sweet Grace. Such a timid, frightened little girl when I brought her into my home. I worked so hard to gain her trust. It took time, connection, commitment, and deep care. Through this process, I learned to be patient, give space, and find safety within myself. Grace grew to be the most affectionate and loving of my little angels. To this day, she is the only one of my babies who I've ever had to put down.

Before Grace, most of my cats had died peacefully, usually in their sleep. I often joked that they knew to just drop dead because making the hard decision to euthanize them would shatter me. I'd imagine them discussing between themselves how I would keep them alive way too long because I couldn't deal with the loss. I used to think that about myself, too. But it wasn't true. When it came time, I did the kindest and most loving thing possible by helping Grace to transition without any pain. Although it broke my heart to do it, I knew it was also the gift of being her person—the person she loved and trusted most—to aid her in this way. In the end, Grace also taught me about letting go, impermanence, and the tender fragility of love.

And then there was Zooey. My soul mate. My truest love. I used to say that I wished I could love another human being as much as I loved that cat. Zooey was my heart.

He was a Himalayan and the runt of the litter. He came into my life as a fluffy, gray ball of love with a squished-up face and an infected eye. From the moment I heard his little meow, my heart broke open. He jumped into my soul and was by my side for thirteen years. I wish it could have been forever.

When Zooey gazed into my eyes, it was like receiving a channel of pure love and soul's recognition. I felt like we had done this before, he and I. He was my protector and seemed to be in my life for many, many reasons. One that stands out is how he seemed to have influence over the choices I made in my romantic relationships. I often felt Zooey wasn't going to leave my side until I was strong and confident enough within myself to be in a healthy and loving partnership. To be with someone who looked at me and loved me the way Zooey did.

I remember one time, after Zooey and I moved to Los Angeles from New York, I started seeing a guy from the yoga studio I was working at—let's call him "Dave." I adored this man, and even though there were evident issues in our compatibility, I was willing to make it work. Zooey, however, did not like this guy. I had never seen Zooey recoil from someone like he did with Dave. Zooey would look at me at times, literally shake his head, walk away, and then go hide.

Still, the relationship kept getting more serious, and eventually Zooey and I were spending most of our time at Dave's place. Zooey was not happy. He hid in the closet. He shit on the floor. He coughed up hairballs on the bed. But I wasn't getting the hint.

One day, while I was working at the yoga studio, I had a sudden, instant flash of intuition and just knew that Zooey had gotten outside. My heart was pounding. There was no logical way for Zooey to have gotten out, let alone that I should know he had. But I *did* know. There was no doubt in my heart, and I needed to get to Dave's house immediately.

Dave had been teaching at the time, and as soon as he got out of class I cried, "We have to go home! Zooey's out, I know it. He's gotten out!" I started to panic. Dave lived in the Santa Monica Mountains, full of coyotes and other predators, and I knew there was no way Zooey, an indoor cat from birth, could survive out there.

Of course, Dave looked at me incredulously and said, "How would you know this? He couldn't have gotten out. The house is locked up. He's fine. You're being nuts."

"No," I said, "Zooey is not fine. We have to leave *now*!"

I was shaking the whole drive up the mountain, knowing that Zooey could be gone. Once home, I ran to the closet he liked to hide in, but he wasn't there. Calling for him, running from room to room, I finally saw an open window. I immediately climbed through the window, tears streaming down my face, knowing that either I'd never see Zooey again or I'd find his mutilated carcass.

I was deep within the property, climbing through trees and brush, calling Zooey's name, crying for him again and again. Finally, I just dropped to my knees and started to bawl. Zooey was gone. After a moment, I stopped crying, took a breath, and, with an utterly calm knowing, looked to my left. There in the bushes, sitting still and just staring at me, was my Zooey.

I looked at him, and he looked right at me. His green eyes were calm, clear, and direct. In that moment, in the same way I had known Zooey got out, I also knew I had to leave that relationship. Dave was not my person, and I was wasting my time. It was as if Zooey were telling me, "You're not supposed to be here, and I'm not staying either."

I left the house that night and brought Zooey back to our own apartment down in West Hollywood. I promised him I wouldn't take him back to Dave's again, and my relationship with Dave was over shortly after that. The relationship wasn't right for me at all, and I would have expended a lot of time and energy trying to make Dave "see" me the way I needed and should always be seen. Zooey had helped acknowledge what I hadn't been able to, tapping into my consciousness and giving me the clearest sign he could in his little kitty way.

It was always like that with Zooey. He was my little man. I always had a sense that he was here to watch over me until I was mature and grounded enough to really take care of myself. To be in relationships that wouldn't undermine who I was in any way. I did a lot of work on myself in the years that Zooey was with me. He would lie near my yoga mat when I practiced and often curl up on my lap in meditation. His fur held years of kisses and tears. He was never far from me and watched me closely as I continued to grow within myself.

It wasn't until I met Al, the human love of my life, that Zooey knew I would always be okay. Zooey adored Al and followed him around with devotion and awe. Al loved Zooey right back. About six years after Al and I got together, Zooey exhaled his final breath and passed away in his sleep. It was as if he knew I was in good hands and it was time for him to go. Although utterly devastated, I was also unimaginably grateful as I watched Al cry openly and dig the grave for our sweet Zooey. Spreading flowers over his body, I gave thanks to Zooey for loving me so purely and for helping me love myself in the same way. That self-love readied me for Al and the beautiful partnership we continue to this day.

I know I'm not alone in my love and appreciation for our feline soul companions, so we invited the contributors on these pages to unpack the complex and curious relationships they have with their own fur babies—as well as the karma that follows. As I read their reveries and love letters, I was struck by how many of us have been uplifted—even saved—by the cats in our lives. Time after time the perfect, weird, and magnificent cat comes at just the right moment, and the relationship that follows takes us exactly where we need to be.

I have no doubt that we are all better humans because of our cats. Time and again they open our hearts, speak to our souls, lead us to our purpose, and wrap their warm bodies around ours. These mystical and precious beings deserve every bit of attention, affection, and appreciation that we can give them.

With that, it is my great delight to present this beautiful collection of odes to our feline friends in *The Karma of Cats*. I'm glad to know that there are so many others who, like me, bow down to our beloved kitties and understand who is actually taking care of whom.

Seane Corn

April 2019

Topanga, California

ABOVE   Frederic and Mary Ann

LEFT   Puja

Radical Respect for Cats

Frederic and Mary Ann Brussat

We flunked the rescue-group foster-placement test. That's the test you face after you agree to socialize kittens or feral cats and prepare them for adoption. When the moment comes to take them to the adoption fair, you can't give up the kittens and you decide that the ferals really don't want to live anywhere else. This is what happened to us multiple times.

After our first two cats, Boone and Bebb, died, we thought we would wait a while before getting new cats. We'd given Bebb hospice care and had not traveled for more than a year. But our break from being cat companions lasted only two months. We found we really wanted fur in our lives.

Enter one-year-old Lalla, adopted from the rescue group that we would soon be working with to place other cats. She was full of energy and ran through our large loft in New York City, enthusiastically jumping up on every counter and piece of furniture. The rescue group advised that because she was a calico—calicos can be dominating and territorial—we should get another cat right away before Lalla had claimed the whole place as her exclusive domain. She tried to do that anyway. Over the years, she developed the habit of sitting at the door to our bedroom to make sure no other cats came in. Even if we had wanted more cats to make nighttime visits, she would not allow it. It was just the way she was.

We adopted Charley to keep Lalla company. He took over our home in his own way. Charley liked to move cloth things. He would go into the bathroom and get the towels, then drag them around the loft, howling about his "catch." If he couldn't get the towels, he would take the pillows off the couch, the dish towels from the kitchen, any scarfs we didn't hang up, the stuffed animals in our bedroom, and more. We told our guests to close their suitcases or else Charley would unpack for them overnight.

Yelling at Charley as we took cloth things out of his mouth made no difference. Figuring that this odd behavior made him happy, we tried interrupting him, petting him, and lavishing him with gentle words. He still started each day by walking around the loft looking to see if there was anything he could move. We closed the bathroom and closet doors and put the dish towels and pillows away. We decided to just live with Charley the way he was.

Julian was only sixteen weeks old when Mary Ann trapped her in her hairdresser's backyard in Spanish Harlem. She was already scared of humans, and the vet predicted she would always be feral. But we were determined to turn her around. We put her in a large cat playpen and gradually, over several months, got her used to us being around. (Our office was in the loft.) One day Julian allowed us to pet her with a stick; a couple of weeks later we could use our hands. One day she came up to the door of her playpen and seemed to be asking for more affection from us. Eventually we let her out to join the other cats. Julian never became a lap cat, but she was no longer afraid of humans. She was not demanding of us or the other cats. Sometimes she hung out with several of them; often she found her own space for a nap in the sun.

Merton was perhaps the most adoptable of any of our foster cats. He was so handsome! He was rescued from the streets of Hoboken, New Jersey, at six months old, but for some reason he was not really feral. He was easy to socialize just by playing with him. We fully intended to get him a new home, but every time we got him ready to take to an adoption event, he would wrap his tail tight around his body, give us that "what?" look, so we just didn't go. Merton was a character. Long-haired with a big-jowled face, he weighed nearly twenty pounds and liked to sit on the back of our chairs while we were watching movies. Sometimes that meant he sat on a guest's head; nobody ever seemed to mind.

Tara, an all-black cat, and Boots, a tuxedo, came to us at the same time. Neither could be touched, and Boots would try to bite you. They lived in the cat playpens for months while we tried to convince them that we could be trusted. Tara accepted her new situation quite readily, and we thought we could get her adopted easily. After all, she would sit in one of our laps and purr. But Tara had other ideas. Every time someone was due to meet her, she disappeared. We had lots of black bookcases, and she'd hide someplace in one where we just didn't see her. After the fifth time this happened, we decided hiding was Tara's way of telling us she wanted to live with us.

Boots was a harder case. She was with us for fourteen years, and we were never able to pick her up. Taking her to the vet required a long chase, many threatening hisses, and finally covering her with a towel so we could put her in a carrier. Yet Boots seemed in all other ways to be very happy. She liked other cats, and by the time she came to live with us, there were plenty of feline companions for her.

> Our cats have reminded us that not only are they signs of Spirit in our lives, they are not under our control.

Boots's favorite was Clare, a Maine Coon cat with a very nurturing nature. All the cats got along with Clare, and much to Lalla's dismay, she was really the top cat in the household. Boots followed her around and snuggled into her lap to nap. After Clare died, Boots kept looking for her. That relationship taught us a lot about how animals can bond with each other. We respected Boots's solitariness and admired her deep relationship with Clare.

Nur also benefited from Clare's ministrations. She came to us having been rescued from the streets of Newark where she was either abused or had suffered a bad fall as a kitten. As a result, she had seizures all her life. We gave her herbs, which mitigated the seizures for years, and then drugs. But it was Clare who groomed her and comforted her. Nur had a funny run; she crossed her front paws in front of each other and kicked out her back ones like a rabbit. When she galloped down the whole length of the loft, she made quite a racket. But she also proved to us that even with a disability, a cat can have a wonderful life.

If you've been keeping track, you will have counted eight cats in the loft at the same time. There were two more, for a total of ten.

Pema and Puja came to us as eight-week-old kittens. They were very beautiful—dilute calicos with gray, white, and cream markings. Pema was short haired and Puja long haired, even though they were sisters. Their coats were not the only things that made them different. They had distinct temperaments from the start, and as they grew they became even more different.

Pema loved to be around us, to be petted and held. She spent the whole day on Mary Ann's desk, and because she also shed a lot, we had to clean fur out of the keyboard twice a week. She was not particularly interested in the other cats. She wanted a human!

At first we thought Puja was just shy—or resistant to us because we had to give her medicine for an upper respiratory infection when she was very young. But as the years went on, we discovered that Puja would best be called a hermit. She liked to be alone, away from both the other cats and us. She claimed the little house at the top of our cat tree as her territory, and she spent most of the day up there.

When we moved from New York City to California, only Puja, Julian, and Merton were still alive of our big cat family. We got a new cat tree with a house on top, but Puja never went up there. We placed an enclosure behind the couch on our screened-in porch, and she made that her new hermitage.

Sometimes we wish we could pull her out of her introversion—especially now that Julian and Merton have died and she's the only cat in the house. But if we set out on a campaign to change her, she would have no quality of life and neither would we. She is who she is.

In our book *Spiritual Literacy*, we listed some lessons we learned from our first cats, Boone and Bebb. Among them were: Live a rhythmic life. Savor the present moment. Keep out of harm's way. Cherish your wildness. When you want something, be persistent. If you are embarrassed, turn your back on the situation and get on with your life. Enjoy small treats. Keep yourself clean. Take a nap when you need one. Everyone needs a secret space.

Our family of rescue cats has reinforced those lessons and taught us one more very valuable one. They have shown us the importance of a core spiritual value we try to live by: reverence. It is the way of radical respect. It recognizes the presence of the sacred in everything—our bodies, people, all elements of the natural world, and animals. Our cats have reminded us that not only are they signs of Spirit in our lives, they are not under our control. As American naturalist Henry Beston wisely wrote in *The Outermost House*, animals should not be measured by human standards: "In a world older and more complete than ours they move finished and complete, gifted with extensions of the senses we have lost or never attained, living by voices we shall never hear. They are not brethren, they are not underlings; they are other nations, caught with ourselves in the net of life and time, fellow prisoners of the splendour and travail of the earth."

To live with radical respect for our cats means letting them be who they are, no matter how inconvenient or irritating their behavior may be. We have lived with Lalla and Pema's gregariousness; Charley's cloth addiction; Clare's motherliness; Nur's awkwardness; Julian's, Merton's, and Tara's individuality; and Boots's and Puja's shyness. As we have adjusted to the cats' natural ways, we have asked ourselves which of our behaviors and character qualities are essential to who we are and which can and should be changed. Such reflection is always a good spiritual practice.

Radical respect for our cats means we don't impose our expectations upon them. We don't try to make them into something they are not. If we let them into our home, then our home must change to accommodate them. If we let them into our hearts—if we really take the time to watch them and listen to them—we will see what it means to live an authentic life.

Our cats, just by being themselves, have encouraged us to express our own uniqueness. They have taught us what it means to honor our true selves.

ABOVE Damien and Baby

Baby's Purr

Damien Echols

When I walked off of death row, I thought that everything was going to be aces. That once I no longer spent my days locked in a cell, waiting to be murdered by the state, I'd live happily ever after. Unfortunately that didn't happen. I didn't take into account the effect that nearly twenty years in a cell, stuck perpetually in fight-or-flight mode, does to the psyche.

The day I walked off of death row, I was utterly destroyed. Within the first two years of my release I had two nervous breakdowns. I was emotionally, psychologically, and spiritually so depleted from the simple act of survival that I had no energy left to even interact with people. They meant the best as they would tell me stories about how they had heard of the case or how thankful they were that I was out—but I couldn't take any of it in, and for the most part the world was a blur of words and faces that I couldn't even retain.

Eventually the exhaustion and internal hell became so much that I could no longer even pretend to follow mundane conversations or remember anything—I would introduce myself to the same person repeatedly, even if they had already told me we'd met before. I felt like I was doing all I could just to carry out the rituals of society, saying things like "I'm great, how are you?" But there were no reserves inside me that actually allowed me to take in their answer—it was more like the repetition of a parrot.

I had no friends. I couldn't relate to the things out here that people talked about—things like television shows or concerts. I was like an alien who had been dropped off in a new world and just expected to find his way with no clues. Needless to say, this didn't exactly make it easy to develop meaningful friendships.

I was alone a great deal, which to me was easier than the alternative—being around people who had nothing within their frame of reference that would allow me to make a real connection with them. It was just too difficult and draining to pretend I was interested in conversations about things like how much the price of parking had increased in New York City.

This is the state I was living in when I found Baby. She was starved nearly to the point of death—I could see every bone in her body. She was caked in filth and audibly wheezing from a serious respiratory infection. She was eating old rice out of a garbage can. Her eyes were as green as emeralds and looked out at the world with wary caution. This kitten had seen great hardship, and I immediately knew she was mine. As I pulled her from the garbage, she was too weak to even fight or try to run.

I carried her home, and for the next several days she camped in the bathroom. I'd go in and sit on the bathroom floor with her for hours at a time. She'd lie on my lap, purring loudly and wallowing on me as if she hadn't been touched in years. We spent entire days like that before she began venturing out of the bathroom.

Baby is highly intelligent and could tell when I was having hard times. There were days when I'd lie in bed for hours, sometimes with tears running down my face and at the end of my ability to cope. And there would be Baby, lying on top of me and purring—a constant loving presence. She would remind me that she needed me to keep going, if not for my own sake, then for hers. And I did.

Gradually, as the years passed, I began to slowly recover enough to once again pick up the practice of magick. Lao Tzu once famously said that the journey of a thousand miles begins with a single step. And so did my path to healing. Before I walked out of prison I was practicing magick for up to eight hours a day. After I was released, my psyche was so shattered that I couldn't even manage eight minutes. So . . . I did what I could and let go of the anxiety about what I couldn't. It began with a single minute of breath work—inhaling energy into my energy centers, lighting them up for at least one breath each, so that they could begin the process of repairing themselves.

And gradually, about six years after my release, I began invoking angels again. At first just a single one—perhaps an angel of the planetary energy Mercury, to aid me with eloquence and the ability to effectively convey ideas to whomever I was talking to when I went to an interview. It was very much like having to retrain a limb with physical rehabilitation, but not only could no one help me, they couldn't even see what I was doing or going through. However, when I was on death row, my firsthand experiences had showed me one thing again and again and again—that magick would never fail me. And that held to be just as true on the outside world as it had been on the inside world. Especially the angels. As I passed the mile marker of my seventh year out of prison, I worked my way back up to invoking hundreds of angels a day once again, which takes me anywhere from three to five hours.

One of the most important things I learned during the process was to approach life out here as Michelangelo approached his artwork. When someone asked him how he carved his sculptures, he said that he just chiseled away whatever part of the stone wasn't part of the figure. That's how I approached life in the outside world—by slowly chiseling away at whatever did not nourish me spiritually. Relationships, places, whatever—if it did not elevate my mind and soul, it was carved away until only the parts through which divinity spoke to me were left. And in the end, that's what healed me.

> In her silence she did for me what people could not—just sat with me, "holding space."

Throughout all this time, Baby was healing right along with me. She sits in my temple space as I do hour after hour of angelic invocations, absorbing nearly as much of the energy as I do. Her bed lies right next to my altar. Both of us have come further than I ever believed possible.

All things considered, the road to recovery has taken less time than I thought. The hard part of that journey was taking the first step.

Baby has helped nurse me back to health as surely as I did her. In her silence she did for me what people could not—just sat with me "holding space," as some would say. Like a tiny monk with only four teeth left, she sat vigil against the darkness.

ABOVE Andrew and Jade

Light of the Lion

Andrew Harvey

first fell in love with cats because of my grandmother, who surrounded herself with extraordinarily strange and mysterious creatures called Siamese cats. I didn't myself possess a cat until my forties, when my husband, Eryk, insisted that we have a child. It was the experience of that first cat that completely changed my understanding of who cats are.

Purrball was a miraculous being. She loved me with her whole being and would lie on my chest after I came back exhausted from trying to raise the dead in Idaho. And she would purr through my chest into the depths of my heart center, and I realized that she was quite consciously healing my ragged, battered, lacerated heart, because ten minutes later I would feel completely renewed.

I started to notice that whenever I was in a state of profound meditation, she would immediately be attracted to come and lie in my lap, as if she knew exactly what level of consciousness I was in and was so damn grateful that I was eventually joining *her* in that state. I also had the most extraordinary experience with her while I was writing my wild book, *The Direct Path*. In it, I really laid down the gauntlet to the religions and to the guru system and said, "Look, human beings have a direct connection by virtue of original blessing of divine consciousness, and the religions and the gurus have exploited this connection with disastrous results."

I knew in a sense that it was true, but it was so revolutionary to proclaim it as *the* truth for a universal mysticism and for the future of humanity that I was trembling in the depths of myself. And one day when I finished the book, I was alone in our house in Las Vegas, and I laid down on the floor and prayed to the Mother to give me a sign that this was not a febrile fantasy born out of my own disastrous experience with a guru, but the reality of what she wanted. And being me at the time, I thought that there would be a flash of lightning that would write "Yes!" in the sky, or a clap of thunder that would speak, like in the Upanishads.

That wasn't at all what happened. I wandered about the house praying and suddenly looked up on the stairs and there was Purrball, glowing in divine light, almost smiling. And so, that was my sign. That in the depths of ordinary life, where there is love, there is God present, and that was an experience that changed my life.

And from those three kinds of experiences I came to understand why cats were adored by the Egyptians. They're astonishingly psychic, they're astonishingly attuned to the higher states of mystical awareness, and they're astonishingly secure, confident, and radiant in their own embodied being. Which makes them, as far as I'm concerned, teachers. Teachers on the level of any of the great teachers. This set of realizations altered what I had understood to be the relationship between human and animals, and that relationship was forever transfigured.

A few years later, a great friend of mine had bought land to protect the white lions in Timbavati, a land reserve in South Africa, and I went to stay with Linda Tucker and Jason, her consort, to visit these creatures. I was initially wary of the extraordinary and extravagant claims that Linda had made for the white lions as supreme incarnations of divine truth and divine consciousness on Earth to give the message of unity and justice and love out of the heart of nature. I was very skeptical of these claims until I myself started to have the most astonishing experiences with them and from them.

I came to a passage at about two o'clock in the morning where Linda claimed that the white lions were sent in spirit form from the binary star system of Sirius. And this struck me as so insane, but also so potentially amazing, that I went out into the night sky. I gazed up at Sirius and I prayed with tremendous intensity and real sincerity to be shown now, directly, if that was true. And at the moment that I made that prayer, four white lions appeared at the gates and roared at me.

The second experience came a bit later but was very transformative. The king of the white lions, called Mandla, was a special favorite of mine, and that's putting it mildly. He was the grandest, most regal being, apart from the Dalai Lama, that I've ever met on this planet. He'd been through everything—kept in captivity for ten years, then released—and now was ruling his land with true kingly authority.

I went to visit Linda about four years after this first experience. My gallbladder exploded in the morning, and I was rushed to a clinic in a place called Tzaneen. I was on the edge of death; I just managed to escape dying because a half-drunk Afrikaner doctor turned up and said, "I'll save you, God knows why," and did. I then returned to the camp and found Mandla himself had been in a fight with another lion over one of the lionesses and was also being cared for. So I went to see him and hoped that we would have a curmudgeonly, weary dialogue between old battered warriors.

They're astonishingly psychic, they're astonishingly attuned to the higher states of mystical awareness.

That was the exact opposite of what happened. As soon as I came to see him, Mandla came directly toward me; sat about six feet away; gazed into my eyes with his piercing, majestic blue eyes; and gave the most frightening, the most exalted roar imaginable. When he roared, I felt Kundalini electricity run up and down, up and down my body and pound my heart awake. And I heard wordless words that said to me, "Don't you waste any moment in self-pity. You have a job to do. You are one of us, that's why you're here. And if you are part of the lion pride, you do not moan, you do not mourn, you carry on whatever happens."

So I received my greatest lesson in and transmission of divine courage from the king of the white lions. At that moment I began to understand why animals are held in such total reverence by the indigenous peoples, because of course they've known this since the beginning of time, because they lived with animals and have loved and been loved by them. They've been helped by animals, guided by animals in dreams and in reality, and they know that animals have essential and different kinds of wisdom that we as human beings need in order to live fulfilling and complete and harmonious lives.

This has convinced me that one of the most essential parts of our contemporary spiritual revolution has to be a return to this indigenous knowledge. As human beings we have made the most terrible and now potentially terminal mess of the world out of our hubris, out of our separation. Animals are not inferior in consciousness to us.

They have another facet of divine consciousness, and they've evolved different facets of that consciousness in different species and are offering us sacred relationships with them so that we can learn from them to live in harmony with nature. And coming to understand this has completely opened and transfigured my relationship with my cats.

After that experience with Purrball and the experiences with the white lions, I came to understand that I needed to be very much more humble, tender, receptive, empty, and awestruck before my pets. My cats started to show me things—show me how attuned they were to realities that I had not yet entered. They took me there in dreams, in visions, and in moments of ecstatic, tender, unconditional, embodied divine love that over time really helped me come into my own power of embodied love in a way that no human teacher has ever approached.

ABOVE Sketch of Karla and Tommy Tiger by Karla's mother, Kara Hubbard

LEFT Kiku

RIGHT Karla

The Miracles of Feline Empathy

Karla McLaren

I never felt much like a human being when I was a little girl. Humans were loud and confusing, or silent and confusing, or violent and confusing, or pleasant but still confusing. Animals, on the other hand, were my best friends and my best teachers. They didn't confuse me at all.

Throughout my life, cats in particular have shown up when I was in trouble and I couldn't talk to other humans about it. Their empathy and companionship helped me survive pain, chaos, and loss—and their humor, feistiness, and love filled my life with delight.

Some people say that dogs are empathic while cats aren't. That's just silly talk. Cats are just as empathic as dogs. The difference is that dogs tend to be undiscriminating with their empathy, while cats tend to make decisions about who will receive their empathy.

If a cat sizes you up and finds you deserving, you'll receive empathy that's just as healing as dog empathy, and perhaps more so because it's focused on you as an individual.

Two cats in particular taught me a great deal about empathy, emotions, and love. These are the stories of Tommy Tiger and Kiku the Miraculous Bonsai Kitty.

Tommy Tiger came into my life when I was three years old. I was dealing with an overwhelming and painful situation alone because my family didn't yet know that I was being molested by the neighbor across the street. They knew that I was having trouble because I was angry and very hyperactive, and I had regular nightmares. The true cause of my behaviors would not have occurred to them. They did what they could to help me, but it wasn't enough.

Every morning before nap time, my mom would send me out to the front yard to play with water. I would stand rigid and grasp the hose with all my strength and watch the water pour onto the lawn, hypnotized by the flow. In a way, I was releasing into the water—fear, tension, rage, hyperactivity, terror, despair—and down-regulating just enough to be able to nap.

My mom didn't know that the front yard wasn't a safe play space for me; it was in direct sight of my molester's front windows. This daily water play was healing in its way, but also retraumatizing. Not just for me but for the poor lawn that I was drowning each morning.

One morning—I don't know how long after the waterings began—a big, orange tabby cat I named Tommy Tiger peeked through the hedge on the side of our yard and plopped himself down near me. Near, but not too near the water. I don't know how long it took for me to abandon the water play, but soon Tommy and I had a standing date before nap time.

He never missed it. He sat with me, groomed me, let me groom his long, silky fur, and taught me about the world. I could tell him anything, and he listened. I could feel anything, even emotions that humans couldn't bear, and he stayed with me. He taught me what friendship and patience were, and he taught me about emotions in a way that I could understand.

I didn't trust human emotions because people seemed mostly to lie about them or hide them. I couldn't get a straight answer from humans about emotions, but Tommy always told the truth.

After months of daily Tommy time, when I was able to calibrate to his honest and accessible emotions and understand them, I could understand humans and their confusing ways a bit more easily.

Tommy stayed with me throughout the years I was being molested, until I was old enough to tell my older sister, who told our parents.

I don't remember when our morning meetings ended. Perhaps it was when I grew out of naps. But I've never forgotten the exquisite, healing, and lifesaving cat empathy Tommy Tiger provided.

★ ★ ★

Kiku the Miraculous Bonsai Kitty came into my life on a gray and rainy day when I was in my thirties and my son was heading into a long and difficult mental illness. He was pushing me away, blaming me, and isolating himself, and my sense of myself as a mother was filled with recriminations and despair.

One wet November day as I was driving to the post office, I saw something gray and muddy scurry from the side of the road into a culvert. For some reason, I stopped to see what it was. It might have been a rat for all I knew, and it was raining, but I just felt that I should stop. I'm glad I did, because the scurrying thing was a tiny, shivering, drenched gray kitten, perhaps six or seven weeks old. Her eyes were nearly shut with a yellow crust, but she could see well enough to know I was there.

I could feel anything, even emotions that humans couldn't bear, and he stayed with me.

She was frightened of me, and she ran into a drainpipe that went underneath the road to the other side. I ran across the road to wait for her to exit. She did, thinking she had gotten rid of me. As she began climbing out of the drainpipe, she saw me looming and tried to run, scared and furious, but I caught her as she squirmed and yowled.

I held her to my chest and wrapped my coat around her to warm her up, and said, "You need someone to take care of you." She relaxed immediately and cuddled into me, and that was that. I took her to the vet, who cleaned her up, cleared the gunk from her eyes and nose, and found that she had beautiful blue-green eyes and every disease known to felinity. He gave her whatever vaccinations he could and sent her home to convalesce and likely die.

I took her with me to get cat food, kitty litter, and a litter tray, and when we got home I introduced her to my husband and son. They agreed immediately that this tiny little girl was ours. If you had met her, you would agree, too. We named her Kiku, which is Japanese for chrysanthemum (the flower for November).

I set up a comfortable kitty hospice for her that day. I made her a bed out of a box and some towels, and she ate some food, used her litter box, and put herself to bed. She knew right away what she was supposed to do; Kiku was astonishingly bright and self-reliant.

The next day, we began our ritual of Kiku lying on my chest and kneading me with her little paws, so much so that she eventually wore out a number of my shirts. I also taught her to play-fight, in case she was ever able to go outside (we had a number of outdoor cats—they were also strays who were at various levels of domestication).

Kiku was an amazing little being, very self-contained and self-trained, and she had a quick sense of humor. I taught her to fight by making a claw with my hand and holding it over her, saying menacingly, "The claw, the CLAW!!!" No matter what else she was doing, she'd begin growling and fighting fiercely, but never enough to truly hurt me.

She was also very empathic and responsive. She would come running from wherever she was if I called out in a singsong voice: "Kiku, I'm lo-o-o-o-o-nely."

She became a family member immediately, and on a diet of love, fighting with the Claw, drinking the water from tuna cans (her favorite meal with kibble), and destroying my shirts, she got well. But she never grew any larger than a ten-week-old kitten (hence her "bonsai" status) and never put on much weight. She was always very slender, and her hair was thin and dry, but she wasn't in pain as far as we could tell.

When we visited the vet, he would call Kiku a miracle and ask what amazing things we were doing to keep her alive. It was just love and attention, I think, and her desire to be with us that did the trick.

Kiku was an indoor cat because she had feline leukemia virus (among many other diseases) and because her slight build and thin coat didn't offer her much protection. She could see the other cats outside, though, and she spent many bittersweet hours at the window, watching them and wishing she could be there.

Our most social stray, the sleek black Jax, would put his nose up to the window and say hello to her, and she would shiver with excitement; she loved him.

About eighteen months after Kiku arrived, she had been symptom free for long enough that I let Jax into the kitchen to meet her (he was fully vaccinated). Of course, he went directly to her food bowl, but I told him sharply, "Jax, no! That's Kiku's food." Jax backed up and sat about six feet away from the food while Kiku watched him. Kiku walked to her bowl, delicately picked up one of her favorite X-shaped kibbles in her mouth, and turned and threw it to Jax with a toss of her head.

I laughed. How could I not? They had their own relationship. Jax ate the love offering and then ran off to scout around the house with Kiku scampering after him. It was a one-sided love affair but love nonetheless.

Kiku lived with us for three and a half years. She went missing one summer day when I was on the East Coast teaching for a week. She may have been looking for me, or she may have gone out for an adventure and gotten lost. When I got home, I looked everywhere for her. I asked Jax and the other cats where she was, but they didn't know.

I looked under the house and in the sheds and the garage. I tramped through the brush and manzanitas outside our home. I crossed roads, went into backyards, and hiked down brush-filled hillsides, calling the whole time: "Kiku, I'm lo-o-o-o-o-nely."

After a few hours of searching, I ended up on a hillside in an undergrowth of trees. I saw a gray blur speeding toward me, and I was so excited. A happy gray kitten jumped into my arms, but it wasn't Kiku. It was another little girl who was so excited to play. I hugged her and loved her, and as I did, I felt the sharp difference between Kiku's body and this healthy kitten's.

Her hair was soft and thick like a bunny's. Her eyes were moist and shining. Her muscles were pliant and plump, and she had what I could best describe as a "moistness" in her entire body that Kiku simply didn't have. It was almost as if, in contrast, Kiku's body was made of dried sinew, fragile bones, and brittle, yellowed paper.

This kitten's presence felt like a goodbye message from Kiku. She had lived longer than anyone thought possible in her feisty bonsai body, and she had healed my broken mother's heart with her immense empathy, humor, and love. This bendy, joyful, fluid kitten showed me that even though Kiku didn't show any pain, she probably was in pain every day.

It could be that Kiku needed me to be gone so that she could take her final journey. I sat crying and laughing with this goofy gray girl for a while, and then I told her I had to go. Just like that, she gamboled and bounded down the hill to a nearby house, and I got up and walked home alone.

We never found Kiku's body. I hope she found a quiet and safe place in which to hide and eventually die. I hope it didn't take too long and that she didn't feel too hungry or too lonely. And I hope she knew how grateful I was—and still am—for her miraculously healing cat empathy.

ABOVE Jeff and Minu

Sleeping with Cats

Jeffrey Moussaieff Masson

t is true that what I have to say here is not unique. But I can't stop thinking about how extraordinary a thing it is that we get to sleep with cats. I mean, that they allow us to sleep with them and seem to get as much pleasure from it as we do. Their perfect little bodies slip into position and mold themselves to our bodies, and then they begin that trick they have of making a rhythmic sound we call purring, which has a miraculous healing power—acknowledged as such by medical authorities—and soon they are sleeping. Do you have problems going to sleep? Get a cat. Better than any sleeping pill. No side effects either, except you will soon be addicted and find you cannot sleep without a cat in your bed. There are worse addictions.

So what is it about this common arrangement (more than half of all cat people say they enjoy sleeping with their cats) that never ceases to astonish us? I think I have found the answer. It is not just that it is immensely pleasurable for us at a physical level. It is something deeper. It is that we are given absolute proof that we have passed some test of reliability.

The cat has decided we are safe, that she can relax into our sleeping pattern and go to bed knowing that no harm will come to her. Think of it: cats are hypervigilant. As wild cats in Africa, they had to find places to sleep or rest where they could be sure no enemy was lurking. Cats have trust issues, no doubt, given how vulnerable a kitten is. Then they found us. We're not exactly the most reliable species on the planet, but once a cat makes the decision that we are okay, they develop a deep and almost puzzling trust in us.

They purr when they see us, they allow us to stroke them, and best of all, they seek our bed when they want to sleep somewhere safe, warm, and cozy. They even adjust their breathing to ours, and pretty soon it's as if two members of the same species are relaxing into deep sleep together. Are the body-memories that of mother and child? Or that of fellow siblings? Whatever it is, everyone lucky enough to have as a sleeping companion a miniature tiger feels privileged, indeed, honored.

How did this come about? Basically there are only two animals on earth who sleep with us as if we are family: dogs and cats. (And by the way, if you want the ultimate pleasure, one of the greatest on earth, sleep with your dog and cat together.) We can love horses or birds or any wild animal we have tamed, but the chances of that animal closing its eyes in complete trust with us is remote. Yet cats and dogs do this every night. Is it purely a function of thousands of years of domestication? It must be more than that. Pigs and chickens and ducks and sheep and cows and goats have all been domesticated longer than cats, but none of them will sleep with us in harmony. Somehow, different from all other animals, dogs and cats have looked at us, decided we are trustworthy, and have thrown in their lot with us. To the point of wanting to share our beds. It is one of the few things that makes me proud to be human!

My most intense experience of sleeping with a cat happened in Auckland, New Zealand, where I lived with my wife, two boys, and an assortment of animals, including several cats. One of them, Meghala, was a champion sleeper. He would lie in wait by our bed, eager to jump up once we made it clear we were going to sleep, and then worm his way under the covers and begin his own little sleep ritual.

He had the softest fur, and he must have known it, because he would stretch his little body out full length, begin his raucous purring, plop his head down next to mine, reach a paw up to touch my cheek as in a gesture of "good night," and he was off to a sound sleep. Sound did I say? Not quite. For as soon as one of our other cats, Moko, would jump up and attempt to get under the covers as well, the hissing and striking out would begin, and yes, I would also be the victim.

When the cats have scratched me in their struggle with each other, and I am angry, I soon realize that they have forgotten all about it. A few minutes later, they are eager to resume their status as cuddle buddies. How have they let go of their anger so easily? Cat's philosophy is superior to mine.

They teach me the glory of letting go of annoyance, as well as anger, and accepting each moment as it comes, with no resentment. Because in fact the past is just that, it's over, and we have important sleep to catch up on together. Why waste any time? Life is short enough. The only resentment I can have is that cats' lives are shorter than ours. How I wish we could continue this journey always together.

Everyone lucky enough to have as a sleeping companion a miniature tiger feels privileged, indeed, honored.

Alas, our love may feel immortal, but we are both mere mortals. This is what makes sleeping with cats so delicious: we know that it goes against their feline nature, and yet so much pleasure do we give them that they do not want to leave us even for one night! They appear to love us more than their own species. Do we deserve such love? Best not to ask, and simply take the gift that cats offer us. As often as possible. At night.

LEFT Ariyeh

RIGHT Rachel

BOTTOM Fancy

The Gift of Cats

Rachel Naomi Remen

My friend who breeds Maine Coon cats lives with her extended family and nineteen of these exquisite and magical creatures. Soon after I met her, her mother, who like me is in her eighth decade, asked me if I thought that cats had souls. A wonderful question. I thought about this for a long time and never did come to an answer.

But the question itself was a gift. It enabled me to discern what I believe to be true. That cats are here because we have souls. Anyone who has lived with a cat can, with a little reflection, discern that their spiritual capacity has been evolved, refined, nourished, and grown through the relationship. And thereby hangs a tale.

One night when I was fifteen years old, I went to bed living one life. When I woke up a year later I was living quite another. My chronic illness, Crohn's disease, had declared itself in the night and taken control of my future. I had been hospitalized and in a coma for a year.

My new life was a life of physical limitations and emotional distance.

My disease controlled my choices and brooked no argument. I was enraged.

I was young and surrounded by people whose freedom seemed limitless. I hated them all. Over the next few years I became more and more isolated from these others. When you are young the world is a physical place: my peers played sports, they hiked, they ran, they bicycled, they traveled to Europe, they danced all night. I could do none of these things. This sense of isolation and difference presented itself daily in the simplest of ways. My peers drank and ate whatever they pleased. I could eat only seven foods, most of them white. Eating anything not on this short list caused me to go rapidly into shock and lose consciousness.

It is truly remarkable how much human connection and relationship occurs in the presence of food. We meet over coffee or over lunch, we celebrate important occasions with dinners and pastries, we bring gifts of food to each other, and we feed those we love—friends and family. We eat together in restaurants and homes. My food limitations placed me outside of this all.

Today it's not uncommon for eight of your dinner guests to have special and different food requirements. Now it's difficult to imagine a world where we all eat the same thing, or where a party of six could order a restaurant dinner in five minutes without any discussion with the waiter, questions about the components in a dish, or requests to modify the food. But this is now, and that was then. Then it was strange and deeply embarrassing to publicly query the waiter in detail about the ingredients of a meal or specify its preparation or reveal my very odd food needs. Yet eating the wrong thing would cause me to become a medical emergency.

Dining with others became an experience of profound isolation and difference. I frequently saw people look at each other in embarrassment or sit in silent discomfort while I sent the waiter to the kitchen to query the chef or ask for some special consideration. Even worse were the questions that many people who witnessed this exchange would then ask me about my condition. Rather than suffer this public embarrassment, I sat through many restaurant dinners eating nothing. Even an invitation to eat at someone's home usually meant asking them to prepare an entirely different and rigidly complex meal for me. Inviting people to my home for dinner meant cooking a delicious meal that I could not eat. Eventually I stopped eating in public or accepting dinner invitations and ate at home, alone.

At about this time a friend of my mother's gave me one of her extra cats. He was a big, red, five-year-old tomcat named Orange. I had never had a cat before and was concerned that he could not talk and tell me his needs. I told her this and she dismissed my worries with a laugh. "A bowl of water and a can of Live-a-Little tuna fish, morning and night," she told me blithely. Somehow this did not seem enough, so I added a bowl of kibble, a bowl of milk, and a can of cat chicken to the daily menu, but Orange never ate any of these things. After a few months of throwing away food, I stopped offering it and just gave him a bowl of water and a can of tuna twice a day.

We settled into an easy and familiar routine. Every day when I came home he would greet me at the door. I would put my purse in the closet, go into the kitchen, and fill a bowl with fresh water. Then I would open a can of tuna from the pantry, put it in a bowl, set it on the floor, and leave the kitchen. I had been doing this for several months before the day when everything changed.

I had come home as usual, prepared Orange's meal, and put it on the kitchen floor, but for some reason this time I did not walk away and leave him to his meal. This time something stopped me halfway to the kitchen door, and I turned and watched. Orange was sitting before his bowl of tuna completely still. His eyes were closed, and so softly that I could barely hear, he was purring. After a few minutes he stopped purring, leaned forward, and began to eat his food—the same food that he had eaten twice a day for the past five years. There was a moment of absolute stillness when I looked at the familiar scene and saw something completely new and different. Both Orange and I ate the same food every day. But I ate it with resentment and he with gratitude.

> Each [cat] needed something from me that I did not possess, and in their presence I grew large enough to provide it.

Like most of us, I had always eaten for taste, for pleasure, for comfort, for connection to others, for celebration. I had eaten out of boredom or to ease anxiety. But Orange was a cat. He ate because of hunger. His food was not an amusement, it was a Good in and of itself. It enabled him to chase the ball I threw for him, to roll in the grass, to sleep in the sun. To connect to the world around him. To grow. It offered him the gift of life. And this same gift had been offered to me as well. I, who had resented others because they could eat anything they wished, was not hungry. I had never been hungry. I, too, had been blessed with what I needed to live.

Words that I had mumbled for many years at the dinner table came back to me in a rush: *Blessed art thou, O Lord our God, King of the universe, who bringest forth bread from the earth.*

For the first time I understood these words not as an ancient formula but as a covenant, a daily miracle, and a statement of profound connection that binds us not only to one another but to the Source of life itself.

Something that had squeezed my heart shut in bonds of anger and resentment released me. Over time I began to wonder how many other ways my sense of isolation and separation was imposed not by my disease but by myself. Over time, I became truly free.

For the past fifty-five years I have shared my home with a cat and am a different person because of it. Orange, Smokey, Tiffany, Sholem Feivel, Charles, Putnam, Cashmere, Maxx, Ariyeh, and Fancy have each needed something from me that I did not possess, and in their presence I grew large enough to provide it. Frequently these things were higher human values such as patience, compassion, kindness, unselfishness, respect, forgiveness. And, of course, love.

Gurdjieff, the philosopher and mystic, has this to say about our relationship to our pets: "A pet is a little tuft of consciousness that circles a person like a moon around a planet and completes their energy field. In a more daily language, our pets heal us and make us whole."

ABOVE   Suzan and Norman

Not Braveheart

Suzan Colón

Y ou've got to see this cat," Nathan said.

I didn't want to look. It hadn't been two full weeks since we'd lost our sweet D'Artagnan, the world's most agreeable tabby. I'd been the one to administer her twice-daily insulin shots, trying to make them as quick and painless as possible. Instead of running away from me, D'Art stayed near and would even signal me with rare meows when her blood sugar was low. Now I turned around and saw my shadow gone.

My husband and I have different ways of dealing with this kind of loss. Mine is naked emotion, weeping whenever and wherever the mood strikes. His is speed dating on adoption websites. "You've got to see this cat!" he said again, and something about the way he was laughing made me look.

The sweater caught my eyes first. A little red Santa sweater, clearly not made for a cat. And clearly not for this cat, a buff-white Persian with remarkable posture—no cowering, chest out, yellow-green eyes front, unafraid. And then we got to the frown.

That frown! An unmistakably furrowed brow pushing downward over wide, imperious eyes. This fellow was outraged—possibly by his plight of ending up in a homeless pet shelter, but mostly, it seemed, by the sweater. "We have to adopt him," Nathan said between giggles, "just so we can rescue him from that sweater!"

And so, on Black Friday, when everyone else was running to the malls to take advantage of pre-holiday sales, we ran to the shelter to meet Braveheart.

The Santa sweater was still on, but the frown faded away when we were introduced in the shelter's small, tidy, meet-and-greet room. The white cat walked over to us with friendly confidence and rubbed against our shins. He looked up at us in a polite way, as though we might be able to help him. *Nice to meet you. Do us a favor and get this ridiculous sweater off me, would you? There's a good human.*

As the cat met our offer of chin rubs with loud purrs, Nathan and I were given two important pieces of information: one, that the cat had bathroom issues—he didn't seem to want to poop in a litter box, possibly because he was raised with outdoor access—and two, "Braveheart" was his shelter name. Because he was abandoned, they didn't know his real name, or if he ever had one.

Nathan looked at me, resigned, knowing the bathroom thing was as good a deal breaker as any. "That's not going to work," I said. "'Braveheart' doesn't really fit him. Let's call him Norman."

I didn't miss that first bit of information, but when now-Norman blinked at me with the love-me eyes, I was smitten. *Love is the answer*, I thought as we put him into a carrier and headed home. *All I have to do is love him enough*, I thought. *He can change.*

It's a mantra I'd chanted many times before. It's the Magical-Thinking Mantra that goes with a kind of love that feigns acceptance but is actually rather conditional. It's Diet Love, meant to be the real thing but full of saccharine platitudes and fakery. It's the blind, deaf, and most certainly dumb (ignorant, not mute) idea of love that belongs in the world of memes with generalized slogans etched in chalkboard-style script. Written in that flowing script is a devil's contract outlining that the beloved will change, according to the bestower's ideals.

All my years of studying Yoga and Buddhism gave me this knowledge, as well as the understanding that knowledge learned from books is not experiential wisdom learned in real life. And even though I'd chanted the Magical-Thinking Mantra before—and the boyfriends had refused to mold themselves to my wishes, and the crazy-making bosses made me crazy until I moved on—this situation seemed different. This was a cat, not a person, and he simply hadn't been litter-box trained.

We all experienced that moment of pure love when the cat-carrier door was opened and Norman took his first tentative steps into our apartment. He looked around—Windows! A big couch! Space!—and looked up at me. "That's right, buddy," I said. "You're home." He purred so loudly he vibrated as he walked back and forth under my hand. His gratitude for a home was rivaled only by his relief when we took off the Santa sweater.

> A heart willing to crack open is a heart that grows larger with its capacity to love.

We expected a bit of trouble in those first few days; we got a honeymoon. Norman was a gentleman to our little Bee, the Persian tabby mix we'd adopted the year before. On his second night with us, I came home to find him on Nathan's lap, both of them intently watching *Guardians of the Galaxy*. Norm slept with me at night, curled in a white ball against my neck. During the day he followed me everywhere. He loved attention and gave as much as he got, which was a lot.

And, as advertised, he had bathroom issues.

We'd been warned about the poop—in that arena, Norman was definitely thinking outside of the box—but he also started marking his territory. The theory that he'd had outside access in his old home—could it be called a home if he had no known name and the owner had abandoned him?—seemed spot-on because he always peed near an egress. Logic didn't make it smell any less like male cat pee.

I showed him again and again where the litter boxes were. I did as cat experts advised and had one box for each cat, then added a third neutral-zone box. Norman began to get the idea, or so I'd think. Then he'd find a new, unmarked space and brand it as his.

One night, I lost my temper. "Norman!" I shouted. "Bad kitty! Bad!" I muttered and swore as I cleaned up yet again. I looked his way to say more words that I knew meant nothing to him, though my tone was clear. I was stopped by his expression. It wasn't contrition. His look was, strangely, one of almost familiar resignation.

The next day I called the shelter. The bathroom issues were bigger than expected, I began, but I was cut short by a sigh on the other end of the line, the audible version of the look Norman had given me the night before.

"It's a shame—he's such a sweet cat," the shelter attendant said. "He's been returned a few times for this."

The attendant went on, saying something I didn't hear because my heart was cracking open. He'd been returned. A few times. Like he was an ugly holiday sweater, not the living, feeling being inside it. I remembered Norman's unfettered joy when we brought him home, the way he scampered from one end of the apartment to the other after being cooped up in a small cage, how he'd looked at me with such happiness when I told him this was his forever home.

I imagined that scene playing itself out in different apartments after he'd been abandoned by an owner who had, perhaps, not even given him a name because Norman had likely been breeding stock. I thought of his joy at thinking he had a home and a name, and then, a few weeks or a few days later, being packed up in his carrier and returned to the shelter. Not once. A few times.

Not this time.

We think of things that crack as being weak, but the heart is not a teacup or a steel support. A heart willing to crack open is a heart that grows larger with its capacity to love. The heart isn't meant to be hard, or even strong. A strong, brave heart is a heart that might shy away from chances to love, to trust, to try again even when that love and trust is broken. No wonder the name Braveheart didn't fit him; he'd been willing to trust again, to love again.

"Teach me how to train my Norman," I said to the shelter volunteer in a weepy voice. My Norman. My little Normie, my Nom Nom, my Norman Poodleboots. My cat who went from having no name to having a name for every kind of love I have for him.

He taught me how to love this way, this little boy from a shelter with a frown and a silly red sweater. This love isn't blind or deaf, and it certainly isn't stupid. The heart that cracks open allows in the love that sees, and accepts, the beloved as they are, and acknowledges that maybe it's the bestower who needs to change.

If this were a Hollywood movie, we'd all be living happily ever after with no scent of cat pee. Instead, think of this as an independent film: We are living happily ever after. There's still a little pee every now and then, but there's a lot more love. And Nature's Miracle orange-scented, odor-busting formula.

At night, Norman still sleeps curled in a ball at my neck, his purrs vibrating into my chest, cracking my heart open a little more.

ABOVE   Theresa and Monkey

The Monkey Mind

Theresa Reed

They say that animals often come to resemble their owners. Or maybe it's the other way around. I am not sure where that statement came from, but I would probably say there is a nugget of truth to it. Perhaps we do become more like our critters, or more likely, we simply learn from them.

A decade ago, my husband and I adopted a little black cat from the local shelter. As soon as they plopped him in our hands, he began to purr like a motor. We bundled him up, took him home, and named him Monkey.

This name seemed to fit him much better than his original moniker, Phantom. Monkey wasn't a cat who liked to hide away, and he wasn't very stealthy either. Instead, he was restless, animated, and liked to play rough. Always in movement, he could barely sit still long enough for a picture.

He's got a true "monkey mind."

I hate to admit this, but in a way we're a lot alike.

Like Monkey, I am easily distracted. I blame this on my Gemini ways, but the truth is that's not an excuse for having too many projects running at the same time with all the technology in the world clamoring for my attention. The blips and dings that alert me that I've got mail or texts or other such things keep me in a state of high alert. "What's happening? What's going on?" Or, more accurately, "What did I miss?"

Like a pinball whizzing around the flippers and bumpers, my brain is in constant motion. Sometimes I've found myself amazed that I was able to get anything done at all.

This was even more obvious when it came to my spiritual practice. I can meditate, but that meditation was usually shorter than the wick on a birthday candle. It would burn brightly for a minute or two before quickly getting extinguished. It didn't take much for that to happen either. It might be a sound outside, or a random thought about my latest project, or some other such nonsense. One thing was sure: I found many reasons to get out of meditation as quickly as possible. Often, the cats would be the distraction culprits. My other cat, TaoZen, would insist on sitting in my lap, while Monkey preferred nipping me. This would swiftly end the session.

Meditation practice wasn't the only way these two would interrupt my focus. Writing sessions were punctuated by petting sessions, and cooking a meal required one hand on the spatula while another held a laser pointer to keep Monkey from biting my heels. Disruption via feline was a way of life around my house, so, as you can imagine, it wasn't easy for a focus-challenged person like myself to remain present much of the time.

One day, I was tapping away on the computer when I noticed Monkey staring down a bug. He was poised to pounce, eyes wide, and completely still. The bug wasn't moving. Neither was Monkey. This was a total showdown between cat and bug—and neither was going to move until the time was right.

Fascinated, I stopped what I was doing to watch this duel unfold.

The stare-down continued for a few minutes. This cat wasn't going to flinch until he witnessed a glimmer of activity. Finally, I saw a flicker of movement as the bug slowly lifted his leg. Monkey's eyes widened as he wriggled his bottom. Suddenly he pounced on the hapless bug, and in an instant, it was over. The bug was lying face up, with no sign of life. Monkey sniffed around it for a second, then sauntered away. The job was done and now it was time for a nap in the sun.

I found myself pondering this long after the deed was over.

How could this cat, who detests the house rules and who seems to be in constant squirm motion, remain so deeply engrossed? How is it that Monkey was able to deftly finish his work while I sat at my desk, still stuck on finding the first opening sentence for my latest project?

The truth was staring me in the face as the little familiar beep that alerted me to an incoming text pulled me away from my work.

I had created a maelstrom of technology and distraction around me. This was preventing me from effectively "killing the bug." If I was going to be prolific, effective, and calm in both my work and my spiritual practice, I needed to set myself up for success. It was time to commit to making my world distraction-free so I could tame my own monkey mind.

This began by taking mindful inventory of what was getting in the way of meditation and work. Of course, there were the obvious rascals: my cell phone, the internet, and, of course, the cats.

I started by shutting the door when it was time to meditate. This ended the cat shenanigans and gave me the space I needed to sit quietly. No longer was I subject to demands for petting or the shock of sharp teeth digging into my hand. I could sit for as long as I'd liked, and my meditations became deeper and more profound. Sitting was a pleasure instead of a chore. This made it easier for me to commit to the practice.

How could this cat, who detests the house rules and who seems to be in constant squirm motion, remain so deeply engrossed?

The next step was dealing with the office disruptions. My new habits involved turning the cell phone on silent and shutting down my email, as well as my browser, so I wouldn't be tempted to check that text or see what was happening on the news. (I'm a terrible news junkie, so this wasn't an easy habit to shift.) I also vowed to myself that the cats would be allowed to roam free most of the time, but when something serious that required concentration needed to get done, they would be on lockdown in another part of the house.

So it began.

A funny thing happened. That monkey mind, which I often blamed on my astrological blueprint, stopped swinging from tree to tree. Instead of constantly looking around at what was happening, I was able to remain committed to the work at hand. As with my meditation practice, there were no more excuses or distractions. I was in the moment, all the time.

I began to live and work *fully present*.

Suddenly, so much of my previous life seemed as if I was rushing through things, never in the now, always on to the next thing, the glittery object. How many things did I miss when my mind was whirling around like a carnival ride? Where could I have shown up better? I'll never know the answers to those questions, but I do know that since I made these changes, I'm a lot more aware.

I've also begun to notice the other ways taming my monkey mind has benefited my life. I listen more and talk less. I've written a book and have a few more that are coming close to being completed. Books that lay around begging me to read them have been finished and tucked away, creating space as I whittled the stack. Most important, I'm present for the people who matter most.

There was one more lesson from that bug incident: the art of letting go. Unlike Monkey, this was something I've never been good at. I'm a record-setting grudge holder, and I tended to fret over work long after a project was finished. Monkey held no animosity toward that bug nor did he keep circling around it, worrying about whether or not it was dead. He did the work and moved on.

This is something I have been aspiring to do myself. I still have my moments of bitterness, but they don't last too long. It's easier to recognize the folly of that. Holding on to that vibe is akin to smooshing an already flattened bug: useless and a waste of precious energy. It isn't easy, but like anything, with practice it gets better.

As I sit here today, finishing these words, I look over at Monkey, who is now deep in grooming mode. Each paw is diligently being licked, but there is no urgency in this task. Instead, there is the pure joy of being right where he is, doing his work, and knowing that at the end of this, the reward will be a sweet nap.

I turn away from this scene, shut down all of my gadgets and gizmos, pour a mug of hot tea, and bring my eyes to the screen, ready for the work that still needs to be done. There will be no distractions today. Not in this moment. Only the intention to be present with what needs completion and the desire to do it with 100 percent commitment. Like Monkey, I know that there may be a goody at the end of the job, but I shall not worry about that for now. Instead, the present—only the present—is what matters.

ABOVE Angela and Golden Boy

Cat Tales

Angela Farmer

Cats have an uncanny way of climbing into my awareness and even my soul. They are masters of long-distance communication and body language. If I let myself begin to feel into one of them, a whole relationship starts to build—a communication that goes way beyond words.

In my early teaching days in London, I was asked to shelter a tabby cat after she had been spayed. A friend who made it her mission to find stray cats and get them neutered said that this cat was not wild but had been abandoned. Perhaps her owner had died. I agreed to take her, but only for a few weeks, as I was to leave for America on a teaching tour. Within days, Mimi, as I had named her, worked her way into me—there was no question of her leaving, and my flatmate was willing to care for her during my absence.

Mimi's presence filled the small apartment, and if I was out teaching on the other side of town, I might suddenly sense her presence and feel compelled to return as soon as possible after stopping at the market for her favorite fish! There she was waiting to greet me, purring and snuggling into my arms like a baby.

Mimi slept at the bottom of my bed, but when it was time for me to be up, there she was planted on my chest and purring loudly!

If I was about to leave on a teaching tour and pulled out my suitcase, Mimi plonked herself on top of it with her back to me and sat there, quiet but defiant in her disapproval. Did she think that perhaps I would decide not to leave after all? There is a part of a cat we shall never fully know!

* * *

It was always clear here in this quiet valley of olive trees on the Greek island of Lesvos that my husband, Victor, was not having any cat inside for fear of fleas and damage to his precious antique carpets. I began feeding a shy gray one who appeared on the property, and that is how it all started.

Word gets around in "cat world," and now fifteen years later up to forty cats turn up at mealtime in the summer, and even more appear in the winter when tourists have gone and restaurants close. Breakfast is dry "breckies" that I scatter in front of the house. Dinner is tinned meat mixed with dry food that I serve all along the stone wall in front of our olive grove. At first, as I head from the shed with my orange bucket and spoon, it seems like total chaos—a mass of fluff leaping, running, rolling on their backs in the sandy driveway or screaming and snarling as the hierarchy sorts itself out. Then, suddenly, peace as a multicolored "wool carpet" covers the long wall, every head down and munching!

I never cease to be amazed at the variety of shapes, sizes, and arrangements of colors: the totally black ones, the pure-white fluffy one with two different-colored eyes, the affectionate marmalade-and-white "lover boy," and so many other cat variations of color, size, and personality. Each one is unique.

A sturdy, white female with a powerful presence who belonged to the neighboring farmer chose to become part of our then "little tribe" and became known as Mama. She was beautiful, proud, and intelligent. Most of all she was very loving, and she adored being held. It seemed as though she created an atmosphere of love around her and was definitely the matriarch. The other cats respected her, and young ones often stayed close for her warmth and comfort. Mama had four or five litters during her lifetime with us and always produced handsome offspring. As happens in the feral cat world, some survived and some didn't. We now have at least two of her grandchildren.

In her old age, Mama had cancer and spent a few days at the animal-doctor's clinic in Mytilini on the other side of the island. Mercini, the vet, and her partner were so touched by Mama's presence that they refused money for treatment, saying she was "bringing light and love" to their home.

A couple of years later, the cancer was clearly eating into Mama, and a wound in her neck looked raw and dangerous. I took her again to the clinic. Life for a sick cat living outside was tough, especially in the winter. I was very sad and wanted to give her comfort, love, and warmth at the end of her life, but I knew she would get that with Mercini. There in Mytilini, Mama had her own little basket-bed between a parrot and a hamster in a sheltered area behind the main clinic and was free to roam the neighboring backyards. One time as I was walking through the building to visit Mama, I met Mercini's partner and expressed my gratitude for their care and love. "Oh, no," he said. "We are the fortunate ones. She is part of our family."

> We stare into each other with no words, and I feel we have done this for lifetimes.

As she became progressively worse and was surely in pain, Mama stayed mostly inside the reception area, which was stocked with all kinds of animal foods, collars and leads for dogs, and toys and medications. It was also home to a few seriously injured animals whom Mercini had adopted. One tiny dog ran around on a support with two wheels, having lost its back legs in a shooting incident.

Mama sat next to the cash register, and apparently many people looked in horror at the cancer wound in her neck. But Mama simply oozed love. Mercini told me that after a while those same people came with little gifts for her! "She is teaching people how to be human," she said.

A few weeks later, Mercini called to say that it was time now for Mama to go, as it seemed the cancer had spread to her brain—she was sleeping on a cactus plant! It would be arranged for the weekend. I tried to feel out and connect to my beloved friend, but nothing happened. On Monday another call came from Mercini: "Mama disappeared, so probably she is not ready yet!"

Two weeks later I had been feeling very sad that due to my teaching commitments it had not been possible to get back to Mytilini to say goodbye to this beautiful soul who had become such a part of me. I started to write my feelings into a letter to Mama as the tears flowed.

Mercini called and said, "Mama passed away peacefully in my arms yesterday, and we buried her in the front garden where only my personal, beloved friends are buried."

When I look at all the cats here, I am in total awe—of their beauty and their agility but mostly the emotions so clearly expressed in a gesture or movement. There is playfulness and sometimes aggression, jealousy, fear, pride, but also love and tenderness as they sometimes snuggle up and wrap their tails around each other.

* * *

My latest love affair is with a magnificent male tabby who always comes to sit on the ledge outside the window just above where I prepare the cats' evening meal. He looks in at me silently with big green eyes that seem to see right into my soul.

His tiger markings in black and gray are exquisite, his whiskers white and long. I call him Beautiful Boy and talk a little to him. He goes all coy and drops his head, pressing it into the mosquito netting over the window. I ask him to show me his mouth, and he yawns, revealing a crimson cave I could dive into, his thin white teeth shining. We stare into each other with no words, and I feel we have done this for lifetimes. He soaks it up, and I feel his love. I am filled with sweetness. We keep searching into each other's eyes—he seems hungry for this contact. It's strange how close two souls can get—a secret I feel blessed to share with this great cat and all the others who have come into my life.

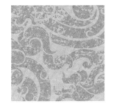

ABOVE Sterling and rescued kitten

You and I, Rick James

Sterling "TrapKing" Davis

Growing up with physical abuse, drug abuse, and dealing with constant dysfunction led me to look for outlets. One of them was animals—mainly cats—and the size or breed didn't matter. I love everything from a lion in the wild to the orange tabby with the fat face running around your neighborhood who needs to be TNR'd (trapped, neutered, returned).

I've always been a cat lover and have had a few come in and out of my life over the years. But it's been my feline friend Rick James who's been with me through some of the best and worst moments of my life. This little homie of mine—named after the iconic funk and R&B singer—has probably taught me as much as any other relationship I've been in.

As I battled alcohol addiction as an adult, it was me and Rick James. In my bathroom I'm throwing up, and for the millionth time I've run everyone away being a mean drunk. There was nobody left but Rick James and the job I may or may not make it to in the morning. After so many years of a sad routine of work/drink, work/drink, and repeat, I finally got into trouble that scared me enough to go to AA.

In a sense I was scared straight, and everyone was gone. I could say I was courageous, but I probably was just out of options. In any event, at my lowest, just like at the toilet, my cat—my buddy Rick James—was there with me. Every night with the shakes he was there, still purring as if I wasn't the bad person I felt I was. I'm proud to say that I've been sober now for more than eight years, and my buddy Rick James is still right here—hasn't missed a beat! No matter who comes or who goes, he's been there with me.

I believe a lot of times in relationships we can mirror each other. I feel like Rick James has mirrored me over the years and, in turn, has helped me see myself so I could make needed changes and grow into the person I know I can be. At times when I was a raging angry drunk, I could see my behavior and how Rick would mirror me. His behavior would be just as crazy and irrational, as if he was the one drinking all day. "Why the hell won't you just pull it together, Rick James?!" I would question my furry friend during these crazy, unruly times.

Eventually I realized that the only way I was going to get Rick James right . . . was to get *myself* right.

Although Rick never opened his mouth and gave me an answer, he continued to mirror me. Eventually I realized that the only way I was going to get Rick James right, just like the only way I was going to get everything else around me right, was to get *myself* right.

This small but really big epiphany would help me continue to stay away from alcohol and aggressively go after my dreams/goals in life—one being to start my own nonprofit based on educating the community on TNR, the only humane alternative to euthanasia (death) for feral/stray cats. TrapKing Humane Cat Solutions is now a reality, and just like all the other big moments in my life, Rick James was right there by my side when I rescued my first feral cat.

Dealing with feral cats, you learn that it takes a "humble confidence." You have to be confident enough to interact with this stranger who more than likely assumes you have ill intent toward them. At the same time you need to be humble enough to know that you're not in control. It's a balance, and that, in my opinion, is the key to life—balance.

I could probably write a few novels on how much Rick James and other feline friends of mine have taught me, but I wanted to share this one with you while my homie Rick James is in his usual spot—still right by my side!

ABOVE Newman on Rick's lap

At Home with Newman

Rick Jarow

'm in a relationship with a cat! Well, it is more of a *lila*, the classical Indian word for "play" that can encompass a full spectrum of phenomena from divine to ridiculous, and this one has run the gamut. It may sound a bit odd, but it is true. I would never have imagined anything like this. Pets are one thing. This was something else. Perhaps everyone who lives with a cat feels this way, but I swear Newman was unique. What unexpected and inexplicable karma brought our life streams together? What is the nature of this shared sphere between all living beings, between cats and humans?

I had never been an animal person. Yes, I had the requisite parakeet and turtle when I was four or five years old, and so did my kids. But this was different. Newman arrived at a very painful time in my life. My wife and I had just split up. The kids were going back and forth between houses. We weren't acrimonious, but there was a deep sense of an irrevocably shattered family, which had been one of my worst fears.

Ironically, it was my ex who informed me about a cat who had been hanging around our mutual friend's house. Perhaps he had been abandoned and was trying to land in a new territory, but our friend John's other cats would not tolerate an intruder. Cats are extremely territorial. So I went over one day and met him, an orange tabby with long white whiskers, fearsome teeth, and a deep rumble instead of a meow. It wasn't exactly love at first sight; it was more like, "Oh, you've finally come, so come on, let's go."

I brought him home. John gave me a litter box, a little cat-carrying case, and a few instructions. I had no clue. When Newman (as he would come to be known) came to the house and jumped out of the carrier, he immediately proceeded to case the environment and make it his own. He investigated every room, every wall, and every crevice, nuzzling up to baseboards, the legs of chairs and tables, and rolling over the heater grating on the floor. I did not know then that he was spreading his scent, marking his new territory. I went out, bought some cat food from the grocery store, and the lila began.

It did not take long for me to get a strong sense that he had come to heal our family. My kids were totally into him, and after a number of days of debating with friends and among ourselves about what his name should be (Mr. Cat, Rangoon, and Raimundo were suggestions), my son, Oshan, came up with Newman. It immediately stuck. I would like to say it was *Numen*, meaning "spiritual force," or New Man, but he was actually named after the character from *Seinfeld*. We all began to sit around watching YouTube videos of Jerry Seinfeld snidely greeting his nemesis Newman fifty times in a row, "Hello, New . . . man," and Newman the cat seemed intrigued.

From the very beginning, he was clear about the house being his. He went where he wanted to, when he wanted to. I did not know that cats have an ability to disappear, and more than once in the early days I would frantically search the house for him, thinking he was gone. I called my friend Bonnie, a "cat person," and she assured me that this is how cats are. Then, when I would hear him rumbling down the stairs, the panic would release its grip from my heart-mind. It was time for his dinner. I really did not know what was happening, but I was clearly falling for him.

It was evident from early on that Newman liked people. He always made himself visible when friends and family were over. He would watch television with us at night, hanging out on someone's lap or, more often than not, making the rounds from one lap to another. All of us in the house seemed to be developing our own special relationship with him. One night we were out on the porch, and my ex came by. When she went to pet him, he bit her! *Ah, he knows*, I thought. Eventually, however, they, too, found their peace. Everyone seemed to like Newman, and different people at different times instinctively called him "Buddy." When people came over to the house, he was first on the list to receive a greeting: "Hey, Buddy, how ya doin'?" In fact, Newman healed this wound that

I could not. He brought us together in a nurturing way. He gave us someone to love, but it was more than this. His presence made us feel at home and not just people living in the same house.

Newman became the guardian of the house. In the evenings he would sit like a statue on the front porch and survey his realm. I eventually understood that he was offering his first teaching. "Eat when you're hungry; sleep when you're tired," the Zen people say. Well, this was Newman. No filters, no hesitations, no problems, rooted in place, connected to his needs. I felt him telling me, "If you have to practice meditation, you are not *in* meditation."

> I felt him telling me, "If you have to practice meditation, you are not *in* meditation."

I have heard so many people talk about being "grounded" for decades, and I have to confess that I was still skeptical about this New Age mindfulness cliché. But Newman embodied the ground: the way he walked, sat, or flew after something; his curiosity; and his demands. Each of us had our own lila with him. My daughter, Maika, babied him with endless love and cuddling. Oshan, who was away at college or in and out a lot, was his friendly protector. My friend Boo, who was living upstairs and was allergic to cats, learned how to be with him at a safe distance. Newman understood and respected this. And I, well, I yelled at him a lot, the way one would yell at the cutest child, or sometimes like Jerry Seinfeld would yell "Newman" in exasperation. Still, every night he would show up, and every morning he seemed to know exactly when I was waking up, and there he was.

We all became deeply attached. When any of us turned the key in the front door at night he would come bounding down the stairs, giving a high-pitched greeting that was the second sound, after his signature "rumble." The third sound was an insistent "Yaah," which he gave when he really wanted something (usually food) or wanted to draw our attention.

One Christmas we bought him a cat toy, a mouse that ran around and around attached to a wire. Newman got totally engrossed in this cat-mouse lila for about ten minutes and then completely lost interest. In fact, anything you could buy that had to do with cats—toys, scratching posts, cat beds—had absolutely no attraction for him. He preferred playing in the grass, scratching furniture, and resting on people's laps, or on human beds and sofas. Thanks to Newman, for the first time in my life, I actually enjoyed being home and settled in. I loved his mindful gliding walk and his ability to just be—no doctrine, no drama, just being here at home, at home with being at home.

During the following years, I fell into a debilitating and extremely painful illness with all sorts of complications. I was not able to sleep for months. Newman just sat by my side, often through the entire night. Who knows what he was experiencing or doing? I have heard all sorts of stories about cats taking on the karma of their "people." What I do know is that he has been with me through my most difficult and vulnerable times. During this period there were times when I really didn't know if I could make it through. Some nights I felt like I was being constantly electrocuted, and his rhythmic rumble would calm me down and keep me going.

He was witness to moments of glory as well. There were times when, after not sleeping, I would go out and watch the sunrise, which appeared as a radiant resurrection burning through the agony. I would intuit that I am—that we all are—born of immeasurable love. And there he would be, sitting beside me on the ground by the bench outside—in his rhythm, fully present.

Other mornings I would rise early, light incense, play the harmonium, and sing. Newman always came—as long as I had fed him first, of course. With my encouragement, he figured out a way to sit on the harmonium that did not block the airflow and hence the music. I would play and he would soak up the vibrations.

During my convalescence, I would get up early and go downstairs each morning. He'd be there, jump up, and follow me to the kitchen. We were kind of like an old married couple. There was less need to talk. We always knew where the other one would be and what the other would do. After his morning meal he would follow me outside where I sat on the rocking chair with him on my lap. Like a baby, he loved to be rocked.

We developed a "live and let live" relationship. Sometimes Newman would hang with me constantly for days; other times he'd be totally off by himself. Sometimes he'd be off, but out and about. I slowly learned to accept him as he was and to appreciate him in his uniqueness as well.

I really saw him as a kindred soul, an ally, an old friend who happened to be in the body of a cat. We had our differences, but he never stopped loving to be picked up and petted. I remember how amazing I felt as a new parent holding my children to my heart, overwhelmed by their total trust in me. With Newman I also felt this. He knew I was there for him.

Aside from his self-containment and easiness in his own skin, Newman taught us about how to accept life's stages. As he grew older, he was less and less the hunter, and the cat wars in the neighborhood dwindled. His hair became lighter. He was clearly thinner and less mobile. He no longer came to the door when we got home, because he was going deaf. Through it all he accepted his life with grace, ringing the bells that he still could ring. When he could no longer jump up from the sink to the refrigerator, I placed a stool where he could jump up on it, and he did.

Newman saw me through heartbreak, illnesses, and extended periods of self-doubt. He began to take on the persona of the wise old man in the family. He was still our buddy, but in his slowness he carried himself with a certain knowing as well as regal dignity. At times when he would sit and stare in one direction for hours, I could feel him transforming from a king to a sage.

My last summer with him was particularly sweet. I had endured a sudden "heart event" and needed deep rest. So I spent days on the porch rocking with Newman perched on my legs, like he belonged there. I was feeling my heart open like never before: to the morning birdsongs, to the green of the trees with shafts of gold sunlight pouring through. I was so grateful for life, overwhelmed by the beauty of existence and by him sharing it with me. He would jump off my lap in the morning, make his rounds, and then return. This went on every day for three months.

As my health returned, I eventually had the will and energy to go to India for a month. Emma, who was staying at the house with us and "babysitting" Newman, emailed me that he wasn't eating. I had seen that before and was not too concerned, but when it went on for a week, Oshan took him to the vet. I was in Vrindaban, the sacred abode of Krishna, god of divine love, when I got a message from Oshan saying that Newman was very ill and the vet was only giving him a couple more days to live.

I immediately contacted the airline to change my ticket. It cost hundreds of dollars and would only get me in one day earlier, but I did it. It may be the best decision I have ever made. I landed at Newark airport at 6:30 a.m. Oshan was there to pick me up, and he raced me back to our house—it took an hour and a half instead of the usual two and a half.

"Is Newman alive?" I asked. Yes. He was. I brought him out and put him in my lap and held him there in his usual place on the rocking chair. It had been five days. He had waited for me! During those days, Oshan and Maika had been constantly with him, and they had made their peace. Not me. I was hoping that being with him might miraculously revive him. I made a little bed out of a pizza box and put him in it on my bed with me. A few times he tried to jump up, but he would fall down again. I carried him down to the kitchen to try to get him to drink some water. Oshan was there. We looked at each other. No words were necessary. We crouched down and removed his collar. He knew we were letting him go. I don't believe I have ever been so present as in that moment.

Perhaps the last gift of Newman—his last lila—was showing me how to die. Like Laozi (Lao Tzu) whose name means both "Old Man" and "Young Babe," Newman let go into the ever-existing Dao. He had been my shepherd during illness, my companion in music and meditation, my occasional sleeping partner, and everyone's buddy.

I have sat with dying people, but I had never actually seen anyone die. That moment when Newman left may be the most intimate moment I have ever experienced with anyone. That he allowed me to be with him, to witness the absolute truth of this broken-open letting go into what is not known, may be his final blessing. And make no mistake, I have been deeply blessed. I am a more grounded, compassionate, and appreciative being because of him. I learned the ways and values of being present, of being home, of finding joy in the little everyday moments of life. And I believe he, too, was blessed on his way by being with us. That our life-streams met, that we shared this earth-walk, is so precious to me. More than any holy place or person, group, or text, Newman impacted me. It took a cat to show me my true humanity.

It was extremely cold in December. I did not know what to do with his body, so I wrapped it in muslin cloth and put it in the freezer. In January, we had our yearly ceremony. In the middle of the night, I felt his being so strongly with me. We were each other's markers. We had become deeply and beautifully enmeshed. Will we ever meet again, clothed in another vision of what we once had been?

Nine of us buried Newman's body on a freezing Monday morning. Curtis lit a fire to thaw out the ground. Maika carved a tombstone. Oshan stood next to me, making sure I would be able to keep standing. I was grief-stricken, devastated, and I never want anyone to take that away from me, for it has touched the deepest part of who I am. Some may be content with "eternal awareness" and "nonduality," but it is this precious temporality, this loss that can break the heart open, that makes us truly human and truly grateful. So-called freedom pales in comparison.

ABOVE Smokey

LEFT Sandra

Smokey: A Love Story

Sandra Ingerman

I still remember the exact moment Smokey came into my life.

I always wanted a cat—a black cat, to be specific. I have been in awe of their grace and intelligence throughout my life. My father loved all animals, and animals really responded to him as if he had a special way of communicating with them. My mother felt nervous around animals, and she knew if we got a dog or cat as a pet, my brother and I would end up leaving the care to her. Because she worked all day, she did not want this extra burden. So my brother and I grew up without any animals in our house.

On April 1, 1992, my neighbor Scott Morris knocked on the door of my partner's house. He walked into our cool, adobe living room with a carrying cage, and my heart started beating rapidly. Scott knew I loved black cats. My partner, Easy, and I often sat and talked around a fire that Scott would build each night outside of his trailer in rural Santa Fe, New Mexico. We lived in a rustic house next door to him, surrounded by mountains and in the middle of a stunning forest of ponderosa, piñon, and juniper trees. Scott knew I dreamed of having a black cat and, without checking with me first, he decided it was time to make my dream a reality.

I had a sense of who was in this carrying cage, and I was excited but also so nervous at the same time. I traveled a lot to teach workshops, and I did not know how much extra responsibility I could take on.

When Scott opened the cage, this tiny little kitten was shaking inside. I put my arms in the cage and picked her up, held her, and told her she was safe. She relaxed into my arms and started to purr. She had short, shiny-black fur, and I love short-haired cats.

Through our unseen communications she revealed to me that her name was Smokey. Smokey was a bit young to be separated from her mother, but the kittens were being given away. We bonded so quickly and immediately that I did not allow my fear of responsibility to stop me from knowing a love story was brewing. I didn't want to lose this opportunity.

Smokey taught me so much about the power of love, bonding, having patience, and being persistent in going for what I want, how to slow down to enjoy life more, and what it meant to be in deep communication with another species. Smokey never stopped loving me or climbing on my lap, even when I rejected her if I was involved in doing another task. She demanded me to be present with her and to stop losing sight of what was important. I never owned Smokey, I just loved her.

I thought my relationship with Smokey would be short-lived as she disappeared only days after she entered my life. We looked everywhere for her. Because Smokey loved to roam in nature, we figured she'd been picked up by an owl, a common occurrence where we lived. But many hours later, I found her hiding behind our stove. An intense thunderstorm obviously frightened her, and she found a safe space to hide behind our stove. But she stayed there for so many hours that Easy and I truly thought she was gone forever.

Smokey turned out to be a remarkable huntress. She was only with us a few days when I came into the living room to see her playing with a bat. I knew at this point she had definitely learned the art of hunting because the bat was at least twice her size. Over the years, Smokey brought a multitude of creatures into the living room to play with. One day I was at my computer writing my second book. When I write, I enter a trance state and my surroundings become surreal. I can kind of see and hear what is happening around me, but all sights and sounds seem so far away. Out of the corner of my eye, I saw Smokey playing with something on the rug and thought to myself, *Is that a snake?* But I was too immersed in my writing to stop and look. My curiosity kept encouraging me to look up. Finally I stood up and started yelling, "There's a snake in our living room!" Easy came rushing into the living room. First, I performed a shamanic healing ceremony called a "soul retrieval" for the traumatized and beautiful green garden snake. Then we released him back into the trees surrounding our house.

Smokey would love to sit on my lap and play with the keyboard while I was typing. We had to come to an agreement about this, as her typing did not fit into the material I was writing. Where we *couldn't* come to an agreement was about her presence in the shamanic healing sessions I performed for clients. Animals are not typically present because they can be disruptive. But she loved the drumming, the energy that was built up in the room before the ceremony began, and of course she wanted to be involved in the healing work. Smokey would wander around my office until she found the perfect place to sit and absorb the healing energies, while at the same time sharing her own.

When it was time to go to bed, Smokey would climb into bed and immediately start spooning with me. Of course, Easy was not thrilled that Smokey had now taken the role of cuddling with me. She would sleep all night with her warm, soft fur tucked into me. The only thing that prevented this from being a truely blissful nightly experience is that she would inevitably wake up to clean herself in the middle of the night. She would stay in my arms while she was doing this, making it impossible to sleep. And then of course she wanted to play! I never got my way of having a full night's sleep.

I never owned Smokey, I just loved her.

There were times when Smokey preferred to roam outside all night. She was still just a kitten when I found her one morning on a step sitting next to a large, male calico cat. Side by side, they gazed into the distance as if appreciating the moment together after a long night of I-did-not-want-to-know-what. But seeing this did fire me up to bring Smokey to the vet. I wasn't ready to take care of more kittens.

In reality I could never train Smokey to do anything or behave in any specific manner, as she seemed to always be training me. For instance, Smokey taught me to never close doors. She would jump and claw on any door as if it were the entrance into the most exciting adventure. It was cute to watch her cue me when she wanted to come back into the house. Living in a rural environment meant we could not install a cat door. If we did, we would have ended up with even more animals in our house besides the ones Smokey was already dragging in with her.

Smokey would wander out on the land for hours. She loved being outside, but she always wanted to gift us with some poor creature that she was getting ready to play with as she would bring it home. Our front door was a big, old oak door with windows on top, and if it was closed she would climb to the top of the wood and hang from her paws so we could see only her precious little head in the glass. I always knew when she was home, so she never had to wait long.

After dinner, she loved to go on our hikes with us. She would always walk right next to us and never stray. It was quite the sight to watch this sleek, black cat keeping pace with us two humans and occasionally bounding ahead, then patiently waiting for us to catch up. We could feel Smokey's desire to run into the woods for some exciting adventure.

Another precious memory I have of Smokey was how we would connect while I was away teaching workshops. I would often be teaching at a retreat center where I had to stand in a long line after class to wait for a pay phone to open up. Once it was my turn, I would call home. Easy would hold Smokey up to the phone, I would tell her about my day, and she would tell me about hers through purring.

The heartbreak for me was when Easy and I decided to end our relationship. Although Smokey was so bonded with me, I felt that leaving her in Easy's home was best. I was on the road teaching internationally for more than two hundred days a year and really had no way to give Smokey a home where someone would be there for her daily. I felt it would not be ethical to take her with me. But I did continue to visit Smokey, and I felt she understood.

Years later when Smokey had become elderly, she disappeared on Halloween and never returned. Smokey was a being who was so at home in the immense forest around our house. I have to trust that she chose her time to die and found a good place to leave her body surrounded by great beauty.

There is not a day that goes by that I don't picture Smokey basking in the adventure of life and teaching me how much we miss when we don't include communicating with other nature beings and letting them teach us about the power of love!

The truth is that cats truly believe they rule the world, and we are their servants. How wonderful!

ABOVE Joan and (clockwise from upper left) Buster Keaton, Francesca, and Henry

The Cat Who Named Herself

Joan Ranquet

A cat makes a house a home. Once that cat is missing from the home, that space seems to lose its soul, leaving a very hollow house.

Nobody knew this better than the ancient Egyptians. If a noble Egyptian's cat died, the cat was wrapped in linen, lamented over, and had a very special burial. The cat of an Egyptian slave likely had an entombment equal to the cat of the slave's boss, i.e., the linen, the prayers, the milk left out for the afterlife. Meanwhile, that slave didn't have it as good.

Cats domesticated themselves and were worshipped in ancient times. They have never let us forget either point. A quick glance can remind us that at any given time, we humans, and the dogs fortunate enough to live among such greatness, should bow down and chant the "I'm not worthy" mantra.

My friend Jenni called. It was July 30, early in the morning. In a panic, she let me know that a box of kittens and a feral mama cat were dumped in her neighbor's yard in the predator-prolific Hollywood Hills. She thought she had retrieved all six of them but didn't know what she was going to do with all of these kittens in her spare room. Before she even finished the sentence, I said, "I'll take the mama cat. The rest will be easy."

I'll take the mama cat? Who just said that? And then I was in my car, driving over to meet her, and I called my mom and told her I was going to meet my new cat, Alexandria. Who just named my cat?

There were a few hoops to jump through—like the weaning, adopting out the babies, the spaying—but by August 13, that cat was in my home. Under the bed. Terrified. I now was living with a gray, allegedly feral cat whose eyes were bigger than her body and unusually kind. She clearly had been a child bride as she wasn't much older than her kittens!

I knew part of Alexandria's being under the bed was grief—she'd just let go of six kittens. It was shock, as well. She'd just been through a surgery. Yet so much love emanated from under the bed I knew somebody had to be missing her. In fact, I felt guilty for having such love in my house—surely someone wanted her back. But then I remembered with horror that someone actually left her in a box on a coyote freeway.

In no time, Alexandria reluctantly jumped onto the end of the bed each night after I was settled in. And then she must have felt who I was and realized it was safe to be all she could be. "Wacky Cat" became her nickname because she would give me such a crazy look and dart around the house. In fact, this not only became an activity generated from her end, it also became a command so that I could be entertained at will!

Alexandria was a dog cat. She fetched. She had to see who was at the door. Really, I felt lucky to work for her.

And in my real job, I worked from home as an animal communicator. She became part of meditating and animal communication. She literally would look at the picture of any animal I was doing healing work with, and I felt as though she helped with the transmission of healing love. When I taught my first animal communication workshop, she loved that she was the more "advanced" being to communicate with—my horse being the shallow "beginning" animal.

I would let her outside for a couple of hours a day. She had to be home at 6:00 p.m. That was the rule. Not 6:01, but 6:00. She was very prompt, often early. When I would come home and stroll through the courtyard, someone would yell, "Joan, she's in here." This dog-cat had human friends throughout the community.

Alexandria was my feline soul mate. We left Los Angeles and were off for an adventure that lasted nearly a decade and involved moving to Seattle, Denver, Florida, and back to Seattle. Along the way, there was a husband and stepkids—and then there was *not* a husband and stepkids. However, the dog we picked up along the way, Olivia, was a permanent installment.

After the divorce and the loss of my mother, I moved to the Seattle area to a little farm of my dreams. The thought was to set up a place for classes and be close to my ailing father. Alexandria, Olivia, and my two horses settled in. The rules never changed about being in before dinner. She was in total compliance. Although Alexandria loved Olivia, she also loved to lord over her the extent to which she was an advanced soul.

One day—it was July 30—I woke up to no cat on the bed, but there was a dead rat next to the bed. Alexandria was generous that way. As I made my way downstairs, I realized I was in the killing field. The front door was wide open, and there was carnage all the way to the barn. The doors to the hayloft were wide open. It had been windy the night before, but this looked like there had been a late-night rumble between my cat and someone else.

I started calling Alexandria, madly. I was looking through every nook and cranny on the five-acre farm. I headed down a trail looking for her. It was not a good day to lose a cat. There were farm chores, clients, and my dad had doctor's appointments.

My heart sank.

> Cats domesticated themselves and were worshipped in ancient times. They have never let us forget either point.

For days I did everything I advised clients with lost animals to do. My search extended miles. I talked to neighbors; I set up traps and food stations—all of it. For years I had reunited people with their animals. It hardly seemed fair that what I could do for others didn't help me find her. For days I appeared to be three hours, two hours, half a day behind her. She was spotted. Until she was not.

I still continued to search even though there were no signs of her. I was heartbroken at the idea that someone could have found her and that the twelve years I invested with her were just over. That Alexandria might be sitting in someone else's living room. Or worse, that in a moment she was taken by a predator, bling and all.

Back at the farm, Olivia and I were beyond bereft. After two months, we adopted a truly grieving feral dog named Isabella, who was mourning being lost and losing her family. And we grieved together for a while until we were finally bored, and eventually it was time to create the new nucleus of this family.

As the years went by, I continued to look over in the direction of the field where Alexandria was last seen, as though in the full moon I'd catch a glisten of her eye.

Two years later to the day, on July 30, my friend Conleth called. "I caught this feral cat trying to catch my lovebirds on my farm," she said. "I just trapped her, and my husband and I think it's your new barn cat. In fact, he's bringing her over."

I'll name her Francesca, I thought. Who thought that? Does a barn cat get such a fancy name? I wondered about her on the farm with all the predators. I then thought I would keep her inside just to acclimate her for a bit.

When Francesca was dropped off, this gorgeous, feral barn cat walked right into the house with her tail up, funny and confident. She greeted Olivia as if she'd finally accepted her and hopped onto the yellow chair that probably still had Alexandria's fur on it. But it was Alexandria's exclusive chair.

Hmmmm. Not so feral. And I had my suspicions: Could it be? Was it? Is it a reincarnation?

A day or so later, I was sitting on a stool at the counter, typing away, when Francesca hopped up on the stool next to me. She let me pet her. She rolled over on her back as Alexandria always did, letting me pet that tummy. And there seemed to be several little legs kicking away like little fighting cats in a bag.

Days later, while on a conference call, the dogs went missing. Missing in the house. I went into the guest room to find Olivia and Isabella peering into the closet with tails wagging. I peeked in and discovered some little wet, furry blobs. I counted. There were six babies.

I quickly kitten-proofed a space for them, and the next thing you know, the dogs and I were helping this child bride raise her kittens.

I found homes for three of them and still to this day live with Francesca and the three offspring—Queen Latifah, Buster Keaton, and Henry—who at this keystroke are eight years old. And they are definitely spawn of Wacky Cat.

I always say, "The crazy cat lady is the new thirty." And that would be me.

Is Francesca actually Alexandria reincarnated? It gives me great pleasure to believe it. Francesca loves to lean up against the framed pictures of Alexandria.

Beyond getting to move through the karma of this soul's introduction to me in nearly an identical way, on the same date, and us having the opportunity to make different choices (like keeping more than half the babies), I see so many other similarities daily (especially crazy-eyed, wacky-cat sprints). And while it may be true, I also see Francesca's soul's beingness in this lifetime, and I don't hold her hostage to Alexandria's personality. I am happy to be a continuum companion to this soul in whatever form it turns up.

The two-year absence of a cat in my home felt like feline bankruptcy. It's just that Alexandria was such a big presence, and I couldn't replace her. But I didn't realize how empty my house was until I filled it with a cat and then cats. In a departure from their ancestors in Egypt, they live in the present and prefer the linens to sleep in and prayers to be said over them *now*, prior to their afterlife.

And now my home has a deep and welcoming soul.

ABOVE Geneen and Blanche

Blanche, Who Loved Me Anyway

Geneen Roth

When my friend Sally called to tell me that I needed a kitten and, fortunately, her cat, Pumpkin, was pregnant, I said no, absolutely not. I didn't want a pet, I didn't like cats, and I didn't want to love anything that could die before me.

I was thirty-three years old, single, and living alone in a house with a garden, three leaky skylights, and a crooked path to a sheltered beach in Santa Cruz, California. After seventeen years of struggling madly with emotional eating, and being as insane as anyone I'd ever met—I'd gained and lost over a thousand pounds—I'd finally crawled out of the compulsion by giving up dieting altogether. More recently, I'd settled at my natural weight, written two books, and begun teaching national workshops about breaking free from emotional eating.

But my obsession with food was a walk in the park compared to the chaos that ensued whenever the possibility of love walked into my life. At the time of Sally's call, I was in a "relationship"—I use that term loosely—with Harry-the-Rake, a self-confessed lothario, who alternated between wanting to move in with me and telling me I was too fat. I was convinced that my heart was either on perma-nent sabbatical or missing some essential ingredients—the ones that allowed normal people to take risks, to discern the bad guys from the good, to say, "Come closer, hold me, go away." And I was wary of opening to anyone or anything that would depend on me to come through. I didn't trust myself to show up. I didn't think I had the capacity for big love.

Pumpkin gave birth to two kittens, whom Sally immediately named Blanche and June. My mother, visiting from New York at the time, wanted to see them. At two hours old, they looked like wet weasels, and I wasn't impressed. My mother went straight for the white kitten. Take this one, she crooned, as she stroked the slicked-back fur of the shut-eyed rodent, but I wasn't taking anything so fast.

A few weeks later, Sally called and said her husband didn't want a white cat, and so Blanche was mine. Usually I am the one who bosses people around, but Sally was completely sure of herself, absolutely positive that having this pet was a precursor to having a life. So I told her I would take the kitten on one condition: if I didn't like being a cat mother, I could return her in two weeks, like a pair of gloves from Macy's. She agreed.

It's not that I'd never had a pet. My grandmother gave me a parakeet named Cookie when I was seven. She rode around the house on my shoulder, sat on the desk while I did homework, and pecked at my eyelashes when I closed my eyes. One day, my brother opened the front door and Cookie flew out of the house. I cried for weeks. I decided then that the next thing I loved was not going to be able to fly away. We settled on goldfish, but the one we called Tallulah got out of the bowl somehow and flipped around the house. My mother and I ran after her with a strainer, but we couldn't catch her, and she died under the brown paisley couch. Then there was a puppy named Cocoa, who pooped in my father's slipper right before he stepped into it one Sunday morning, and by Monday, she had gone to live somewhere else.

When she heard that Sally wanted to give me a kitten, my friend Sophie told me her pet story. After her mother died and her husband left her for another woman, she thought she was going crazy—the kind of crazy where a psychotic break was two weeks away. On a particularly rough day, a group of friends tried to make her feel better, but she sensed their fear. The fact that her best friends couldn't be with her sorrow made her feel even more frightened, more alone. Then her dog, Squeak, jumped in her lap and fell asleep. In that moment, she says Squeak saved her life. He cut through the drama, walked directly on the fiber of feelings, and stayed there, as if pain and grief were no big deal—as natural as chasing squirrels. His relaxation dissolved her fears of going crazy. After that, she was left with a broken heart, and as much as that hurt, she knew it would mend.

Though I was glad Sophie had her dog, I'd heard these sappy tales before—a boy and his dog, a girl and her parrot, the wolf who saved the family from a fire—and didn't see what they had to do with me. I still didn't want a cat.

During our first few days together I refuse to be charmed by Blanche, although every time I turn a corner, she is there, crouching behind philodendron leaves or stalking an ant or a dust mote or my big toe. When I say no, she doesn't hold a grudge. When I push her away, she comes back. Blanche's affection doesn't waver if my hair sticks straight up in the mornings or if I am having a fat day. She seems to be looking beneath the surface of things at some backward-spreading light I am not aware of.

> She seems to be exactly the same shape as the craggy hole in my heart.

A week after Blanche arrives, my two-year relationship with Harry-the-Rake ends when he falls in love with another woman. Flinging myself on the bed in a paroxysm of sorrow—What will I do? Where will I go? Who will ever want me?—I notice a cloud of fluff inching across the quilt until it settles on my heaving chest, wheezing a low, gravelly purr. It's difficult not to be melted by such total acceptance; it's hard to keep insisting that the world is a terrible place.

On the eleventh day, I admit I am smitten and tell Sally I will keep the cat.

Once I cross over, every single thing about Blanche enchants me, and I am positive that no one has ever had a cat this adorable. Then I start to worry that I love her because all kittens are irresistible but that when she gets older, I won't love her anymore. I still believe love depends on what you look like.

Within a month, Blanche has about ten thousand nicknames: Pooters, Banana, Wig-Wig, Moochy-Mooch, Fuzzy-Wuzz, Petunia, Mr. Guy and a Half, Sweet Potato, Booch Pie, Blue, Moo, Dandelion. Blanchebananche, Peachy Canoe and Tyler Too, Curly-Whirl, and on and on. Every day, a different name.

Within two months, I can't imagine that I've ever lived without her. She seems to be exactly the same shape as the craggy hole in my heart, so when I see her, all my stick-out edges and weird crazy ways smooth down. I feel as if I've been dreaming her for years and now she is here.

It never occurs to me to question my choice of love objects or wish that Blanche were a person instead of a cat. When you've been famished for decades and someone hands you a slice of warm, pumpernickel-raisin bread and homemade jam, you don't ask for chocolate cake instead.

ABOVE   Briana with Hades (left) and Aphrodite

Out of the Storm,
Into the Heart

Briana Saussy

n late August and early September of 2017, the Gulf Coast of Texas was hit by the tremendous force of Hurricane Harvey. In San Antonio, where I live, the storm did nothing more than shed life-giving rain on our thirsty land, but in East Texas, and especially around the city of Houston, neighborhoods were decimated as the flood waters rose higher and higher. Homes and lives were lost. Those of us with friends and family in the eastern part of the state stayed close to phones and made use of social media to learn what was happening to our beloveds and to find out what we could do to help. In a year that had seen the white supremacist rally spread vicious poison in Charlottesville, Virginia, over the summer, the storms of Harvey wrought both devastation and healing—for we all needed to see people coming together and helping each other in the ways that they did during the storm. No blame, no division, just human beings helping each other. Is this not, in the last analysis, what we in truth *are*?

Storms affect more than human lives. Hundreds of thousands of animals were killed or stranded during Hurricane Katrina years before—and many thousands met the same fate in Texas, despite the doubled efforts this time around to prevent it from happening. San Antonio became a haven for many thousands of animals displaced by Hurricane Harvey. Among these was a pregnant calico cat who would, in mid-October, give birth to three kittens, two of whom would survive and find their way into my family's home and life, carrying with them all kinds of lessons, the greatest of which has been one of resilience. Our little boy named these kittens Hades and Aphrodite, and this is their story.

When we use the word *resilience* today, we typically mean the ability to bounce back relatively quickly from an unpleasant event. This understanding, though accurate, barely scratches the surface of what the word actually means. When we look at the etymology we find the prefix *re-*, meaning "back to the original place," and the verb form *salire*, meaning to "leap," "flow," "run," or "hurry." So when we speak of resilience, what we are really describing is not merely the ability to bounce back or shake off a difficult experience. We are speaking of the ability to return, to leap and flow, to run and hurry back to our original place, back to our foundation, back to our deepest roots. We are speaking of the ability to remember who we really are and how to make our way back into the sheltering embrace of that knowledge.

This is no small thing. There are storms all around us—from the latest "if it bleeds, it leads" stories in the media, to coverage of various political upheavals and economic challenges, to say nothing of the personal encounters we have day in and day out that threaten to make the floodwaters of forgetfulness rise up. These tempests cover over our knowledge of who we really are and what we are really about. There are inner storms as well: the critic's voice telling us that this work or that idea or endeavor is stupid and pointless and why bother, the old stories we carry with us concerning every aspect of life—from money to sex to rightful work in the world—that can so easily threaten to engulf us and so insidiously manage to persuade us to ignore our actual experience and instead buy into a phantasm of untruth. Resilience, related to words such as *resistance* and *return*, is the much-needed antidote. It is the ability to remember our original place and to find the path back to it in the many ways each of us possess. In fact, given how deep and fundamental resilience is to our experience, we might wonder: Can a couple of cats really have much to teach about this essential quality? The answer is yes, oh yes, they can.

I stumbled upon the kittens by sheer accident. My husband and I had been thinking about getting two kittens for Christmas. We wanted cats, and the time for them seemed right: our son was six going on seven, and we knew that two feline additions would give him a good taste of responsibility and caretaking. I mentioned to a mom friend of mine that I was looking for a couple of kittens, and she told me that she had two of the sweetest—but there was a catch, and it explained why the two lovable felines had not been adopted by late November. One of the kittens, the female, had a neurological disorder that made it impossible for her to walk more than a few steps without falling to the side. She was also blind and would most likely be prone to seizures. My friend's hypothesis was that she had suffered these ailments because the momma cat was given a full suite of vaccines when she was almost full term with the kittens. In other words, the little lady had been born that way and would have these challenges throughout her life.

> There are jewels to be found in the rubble if you are willing to do the work of looking.

The kitten was sweet and tough, my friend assured me—she had figured out how to get herself to her food and water bowls and how to use the litter box, but she would be a higher maintenance pet. A number of people had been interested in adopting the healthy male kitten, but my friend, the good vet, would not separate brother and sister. The situation was desperate, though, and if it didn't get resolved soon, both would be sent back to Houston for euthanasia. So, did I want to come and meet the kittens? Well, of course I did!

So, weeks after the floodwaters had receded, my husband and I went to meet these unlikely survivors. Hades, with his black fur and constant purr, was easy to adore. Aphrodite had a patchwork, tortoiseshell coat with tufts of fur sticking up this way and that, copper-penny eyes, a querulous meow, and stuttering legs. She looked like she would be a handful, so obviously we both fell in love with her, too. Christmas arrived, and the kittens came home. I thought it was especially prescient of my son to name the little lame kitten after the goddess of love and beauty.

At the time we adopted them, I was three months pregnant with our second child and working on my first book. My mornings started at four o'clock, and Aphrodite was by my side as I lit my incense, chanted my prayers, and crafted my words. Then it was time to tie my apron, blazoned with the glory of Guadalupe, around my waist and give Aphrodite her breakfast. I quickly learned the apron was essential because her claws were needle sharp, and she hung on to anything for dear life to maintain her balance. I fed her by hand, and in the cold winter months that warmed into spring, I realized that tending this little creature had also become an integral part of my practice. As time moved on, Aphrodite's tummy became rounder, and her legs became a bit more steady—and then a bit more.

Aphrodite will never walk as steadily as her brother. But then again, walking steadily is not her original state. What resilience means for her, then, is not becoming a "normal" cat. It means returning back to love, and to love's consequence, shining from her eyes and her melodious call, and flowing from our touches. Both she and Hades provided the opportunity for our little boy to learn to care for vulnerable beings and to learn what it means to be differently abled, not in a hypothetical or abstract sense but from real, observable experience.

As a sacred artist, one of several modalities that I work with is the Tarot. Like many divination practices, the art is typically regarded as a little too risky and edgy for polite, respectable society, even for communities of spiritual soul seekers. Consequently, the Tarot is often ignored. And yet it should not be, for the Tarot—far from being occult esoterica—is, in truth, an age-old art of both divination and perennial insight that can help enrich our daily wisdom and aid us in finding healing and wholeness. One of the most feared cards within the Tarot is the Tower. Typically the Tower card shows some version of a tower that is being blasted by a lightning bolt and falling to the ground. Whenever the card is pulled, it often indicates that something is being destroyed, taken down, or rocked to its foundation. Sometimes this might be a perception or way of seeing certain things. In other cases, the card might be more literal—a cherished relationship might be in the process of falling apart, or the job you were hoping for might be in the middle of restructuring. For these reasons, when many people sit down for a Tarot reading, they hope that they will *not* get this card. What is often missed when working with the Tower card is the presence and power of resilience. For, as I like to say to my clients, there are jewels to be found in the rubble if you are willing to do the work of looking.

It is this way for us, too. Storms do come, and devastation is wrought. But there are also jewels that come out of those storms. Sometimes it is the jewel of finding your way back home—your way back to your original place, to your heart. Sometimes they are the jewels of two furry kittens, surviving in the face of crazy odds, reminding you that the original places for all of us may look different, but they always should include safety, warmth, and love for the sake of nothing more, or less, than itself.

LEFT Basia

RIGHT Biet

The Three Teachings of Basia

Biet Simkin

In the fifteen years I spent with my cat Basia, she taught me that magic is real and easy, that protection and care are needed as we move ahead on our journey, and that grief is an inevitable part of true love. Animals are unique in that they don't care about culture or architecture or real estate, so the lessons they teach us are so pure and unfiltered. They are like infants, walking embodiments of true love. Love, like time, is a dimension outside of reality. My cat taught me, as all true love has, that I ought to spend as much time as possible in that dimension rather than in the 3-D prison we call "life."

Magic Is Real

When I was eighteen years old, I decided to get my father a cat as a surprise for his birthday. Like most gifts back then, my motives were also sort of selfish, as I wanted a kitten myself. I called my friend—this young Italian girl from Queens—who was my neighbor (and she had a car!), and I asked her if she would drive me to North Shore Animal League so I could adopt a kitten. In a heavy Queens accent she said to me, "Why you gonna go to North Shore? We can just go find you a cat in the street." Now I was totally perplexed, although I had seen cats in the street before. They were sort of mangy and certainly not an adorable kitten like you see in those adoption commercials. However, my friend assured me that her grandma was the queen of finding cats in the street, and she and I and her Italian grandma were going to go get a cat in the street later that day by driving around Jackson Heights.

We got into her grandma's car, the three of us, and off we went to go find this impossible kitten. First we drove toward 71st Street and saw a few three-month-old kittens running. We got out of the car and chased one white one, but he was too scared. "This one is too skittish," the grandma said. "It's been ruined by the streets already; let's keep movin.'" I was in the car thinking, *This is truly the dumbest idea I have ever heard of, going around the streets looking for a cat. Who the fuck does that? It's literally Queens crazy!* I did, however, believe them. There was something very organic and easy about the whole process, and I trusted that as weird as it was, it was going to lead to a cat.

All of a sudden, on 74th Street, one block from my house and a street that I frequented, we came upon a house whose stoop was covered with a giant family of cats. There must have been something like fifteen cats, all different colors and sizes, all adult cats, all chilled out and simply relaxing. Then I saw one little tiny kitten sitting on the stoop. Although it was clear that these were all street cats and belonged to no one, it was also clear that, unlike the white cat from 71st Street, these cats had not been "ruined by the streets." I got out of the car and walked straight to the little kitten. I picked her up, and she fit in the palm of my hand. She was no older than four weeks. I placed her seated in the palm of my hand and looked at her face. She opened her eyes and had one blue eye and one brown, like David Bowie. I knew immediately that she was my cat. I said to her, "You are a Simkin!"

The whole mission to find her took no more than an hour. I continued to live in Jackson Heights for the next ten years and never again saw random cats in the street, or a family of cats on that block. It was almost as though a wormhole had opened and these cats just appeared from inside. It was crazy!

This was Basia's—we named her Basia—first lesson to me: when we want something and believe it to be ours, it simply appears in the world. This is spoken about in great detail in the works of Florence Scovel Shinn, Esther Hicks, and also covered in Rhonda Byrne's *The Secret*, but I was years away from having read any of that, and Basia was my evidence. The world is not real. It is a matrix that is governed by our ideas and faiths. We master it with the right use of our understanding.

Protection Is Necessary

Basia was with me for the next fifteen years. I believe she was sent to protect me because, honestly, in those fifteen years we both should have died. In those years, Basia hung around while I slept with one skinny intellectual boy after another. She sat with me on the table while I took shot after shot of vodka. She stayed on the table when the vodka turned to heroin. Heroin that I would stealthily snort off the tabletop. She was with me every time I cried.

I cried a fair amount back then—every time a boy broke my heart or every time I really got a deep taste of all my fears and had no tools to deal with them. If Basia heard me crying, she would run across the entire apartment, a two-thousand-square-foot space, to find me, snuggle into me, and rub her face into my tears. Basia was everything!

She was there when my daughter was born, although she couldn't really believe I loved anyone more than her and wasn't a fan of that. She was there four months later when my daughter died of SIDS. She was with me through that horror. She was there when my house burned down, and I think somehow kept half the apartment from burning so that she could survive. She was there when my father died, and she was with me as I got sober and turned into a woman of dignity and grace.

The loss of Basia is mine, and her gift to me. The loss of true love is always like that.

Basia watched a very unlikely event occur, which was my transformation. Most people go their whole lives without ever transforming. It is such a sad thing. But in my life, I transformed. I went from being a hopeless, heroin-addicted artist who cared about nothing and no one but herself to being an author, artist, and spiritual teacher sharing ancient wisdom with people all over the globe. I went from being near death to radically alive.

Basia was with me through all this. She protected me and held space for my awakening. She was patient, too, because it took a long time to "become real," as the Velveteen Rabbit says.

Grief Is Unavoidable

Basia died. She got cancer and we had to put her to sleep. My then boyfriend, now husband, Christophe, and I took her to the vet and put her to sleep. We wept and wept as we held her and she went cold. I didn't want to face it. I loved her so much. I was never a fan of pain, having lost most of my family to death by the time I was twenty-eight years old. I was just not a fan of "feelings," if you know what I mean. Perhaps because mine had always been so overwhelming to me.

I have since learned that I am blessed to have felt so deeply, and today I actively open to feeling everything. But back then I still recoiled.

Two months after we put Basia down, I went to a pet store in Brighton Beach, Brooklyn, and decided to buy a baby Scottish Fold kitten to heal my woes. It was Christmastime, and I was so excited. I took the train to this deep Brooklyn pet store and found this kitten. The store was weird, to say the least, and I had a strange and ominous feeling. But the love I had for this new kitten was so strong that I overlooked the ominous warning of my intuition and bought her for a thousand dollars, which was the most money I had ever spent on anything. I had only recently begun living above the poverty line, and this was some of the very first money from my work as a spiritual teacher. I named her Pushkin, which—may I say for the record—is basically the best cat name ever!

Pushkin was so tiny, and like all Scottish Folds, had those folded ears that made her face look like a pumpkin. It was painful to look at her because her cuteness was almost intolerable. I thought I had won the lotto. My pain about Basia was covered over now, and the relief set in.

However, this was not a happy tale. Pushkin proceeded to poop all over my belongings and my bed. I thought she was just misbehaving, but no, she was dying of a horrible illness caused by "backyard breeding." This little kitten was badly bred, and she would die a horrible death a few months later at the young age of five months. Christophe was angry at me for making him go through this much heartache just seven months after the Basia heartbreak. This was excruciating, but I think I still had more to learn.

Two weeks later, I was at the hair salon and told the stylist my kitten had died. The stylist told me he had a Persian cat that he needed to let go of as he was never home and asked if I would take him.

I thought this was like a gift from God. *Wow, I lose a kitten and then a big fluffy Persian is given to me.* I said, "Yes, of course!"

The stylist brought him in the middle of the night with no carrying case. (To say this man was eccentric would be an understatement.) We named this cat Mukti, and it turned out that Mukti was a raving lunatic. He was like what you would get if Kramer from *Seinfeld* was a cat. He hid in the wall of our apartment for the first two weeks, barely even coming out for food. When he did emerge, he would just pee on the couch. It was a total disaster.

What karma, I thought! It took Mukti a year to calm down, but once he did, he was a supercool cat. Ironically, he wasn't into me. He hated me but loved Christophe, which is a curse for someone who loves cats as much as I do.

I regretted ever getting him for two more years. I suffered and suffered. After a couple of years it dawned on me, though: You can't avoid grieving. This is exactly what I was trying to do. I didn't want to feel the loss of Basia, so I did all this other stuff, and in the end it took what it took.

Three years after getting Mukti, we finally fell in love. He is a really cool and amazing cat. He isn't Basia—and no one ever will be—but the truth is, I needed three and a half years to grieve her loss, and it wouldn't have happened if I just got another perfect cat right after her death.

The universe has payment as a law, and I paid for my grief. Through the loss of Pushkin. Through the horror of the initial stage of my relationship with Mukti. I paid and paid. When the karma of my grieving Basia was over, all was restored to normalcy.

The real takeaway is that "time takes time." I think she taught me that, and I am grateful that it was all exactly as it was because I would not want to cover up the loss of her. The loss of Basia is mine, and her gift to me. The loss of true love is always like that. May we wear it bleeding rather than try to bandage it. May we bleed and weep openly. That is spirituality. Spirituality is everything, so it is this also. Terrible grief is spirituality just like terrible joy. It's all one beautiful thing.

ABOVE Stéphane and Néo

The Story of Life,
the Story of the Cat

Stéphane Garnier

For as long as I can remember, I have always lived with cats. From the earliest days of my childhood until now, cats have always been present in my life to protect me, listen to me, guide me, and bring a smile to my face.

When I was around three or four years old, I can remember that Sami, our Siamese, would chase away the snakes that would hide under the sandbox my sister and I played in when we lived in the countryside. Then Papouf arrived in our lives. Papouf, an enormous cat, showered us in his love, giving us hugs and keeping us warm with his thick, rust-colored fur. And I couldn't forget Vanille and Noirette, two cats who were equal members of our family in the years to follow.

I soon adopted Whisky—Vanille's son—as an adolescent, and he was the first cat who was uniquely mine, my own. Whisky would follow me everywhere, listening to every one of my moves. He'd stand guard over my drafts and many blackened pages when I began taking my first steps in writing through some songs and poems. Little did I know that these first steps and inspirations would stand to represent my future life and career.

Until I left to do my studies in Paris, my life was always lived together with cats. But it was impossible to welcome an animal who so desired liberty and wide-open space when I moved into a small dorm room for several years.

During this period, there was no longer someone to share my days with. No longer someone to listen to me when my sense of solitude overcame me and my problems seemed to multiply. It was then that I realized how much space in my heart and in my everyday life cats had occupied over all those years. They had always been there to make me laugh, to play, to cheer me up during difficult moments, and to show me their love.

Sometimes, even in the coldest winters of our existence, the cat is there. He's there to warm us, to soothe us. He gives, he loves, he embodies all of life.

A few years later, when I moved again into a small house in the countryside, I adopted two more cats, a brother and sister named Ziggy and Shan. They were inseparable. They became the guardians of the house, my companions in life and in work—especially when I worked tirelessly, late into the night, on my first books.

When I begin to think back, I start to ask myself who was there—outside of my few close friends—in those early years when I debated myself between the lines? Who was there to comfort me when I received those letters of rejection on my first manuscripts? Who was there when I became an unemployed college graduate, desperately lacking money? Who was there each and every day to comfort me when the bills and the bank's overdraft letters piled up on the refrigerator, which always seemed to empty and never replenish. Who was there the day (when I thought nothing worse could happen to me) that my partner left me? My loyal cats. There was still Ziggy and Shan—their eyes filled with all the tenderness in the world—to murmur in my ear, "To say anything means nothing; you must do. And the essential is not just to do, but to hold space for the things to come. We are here, and this too shall pass."

If we could discern one precise thing that a cat can offer us in life, it would be a shared, harmonious lifestyle. When you share your life with a cat, a being that is both so discrete and subtle, you know that even if you don't always see them, they are always still there in spirit. You can sense their presence around you and within you during every minute you spend with them. Even if you think you adopted them, they are actually the ones who adopted you. They've opened the door to their world, a world that shines a brighter light on things than our own. Everything becomes a little less linear, a little less dualistic. In time, we begin to mimic cats, to put their same perspective on our own world. Everything becomes more supple; the angles in our point of view become more fluid. And when you sit next to your cat, your gaze looking further in the distance, you begin to perceive in the silence that the world is full of vibrations and connections.

I had always been fascinated by his sense of nonattachment, of his comfort in letting go.

A cat is not just an animal companion. Over time, he becomes a companion for life, and really, at the end of the day, he is our true guide.

Unfortunately, Ziggy's sister, Shan, passed away at a young age after being hit by a car, and Ziggy alone became my guide. At that point, it was just the two of us. We were a real family—real friends. He could count on me, and I could count on him.

To better understand this close bond between us, there is a facet of our story concerning his paw that I have not previously told in my book *How to Think Like a Cat*. A few months after Shan's death, Ziggy also fell victim to an accident. A speeding motorcycle hit him outside our home. Ziggy was able to make his way slowly back into the house, and I quickly rushed him to the emergency veterinarian.

The diagnosis: the motorcycle had crushed a part of the spinal cord behind his right shoulder. It was likely that he would never be able to use his front right paw again, even following treatment. However, there was also a slight chance that the nerve endings could reform, so I decided to let him keep his paw in the hopes that it might heal successfully. The risk of doing this, the veterinarian warned, would be that Ziggy might not regain any sensation in his front right paw. Should he ever hurt it, he might not even realize his injury and could potentially bleed to death.

Ziggy healed well following his accident, though he never regained the use of his paw. He limped awkwardly and could hardly apply any pressure to his paw. This slowed him down quite a bit.

A few weeks later, though, just as the veterinarian feared, he cut his paw. Once again, he managed to limp home, seemingly calm but covered in blood. I brought him back to the emergency clinic, but this time around his paw needed to be amputated.

I came to meet him after his surgery, and upon seeing me—and to the amazement of the veterinarian!—he leapt into my arms, wrapping his remaining paw around my neck like a child. He felt fantastic, even without his fourth paw. However, the next bit of bad news fell on me when I saw the vet bill for the two visits.

I was unemployed and had no stable income at the time. I ended up having to borrow money and split the bill into five installments just to pay the veterinarian.

This financial detail does have its importance, as I am about to explain. When we arrived back home that evening, I had a very long discussion with Ziggy, explaining to him the current situation we were in.

It was simple. I had just plunged myself into debt to save his life, and if he made any more mistakes during his recovery, I would simply not have the means to pay for his care. I talked to him for hours, and he sat attentively in front of me, his eyes fixed on me tenderly. I wanted him to understand that we had no other choice than for him to heal successfully and to stay in good health for a long time to come.

Since that day, he neither fell ill again nor got involved in any other accidents, although it did bother him that I took away his liberty to come and go as he pleased, something he cherished greatly. But we made a pact that evening, a pact for life, and for all the years that we had yet to spend together.

He healed from his amputation without any problems and went back to his usual life. He continued his activities and explorations without limping or dragging his stump or seeking pity from anyone. His ability to adapt seamlessly to this major change flabbergasted me.

From then on, I began to observe Ziggy differently. I discovered a few life secrets, habits, and talents among the many amazing abilities of cats that we ourselves would benefit from learning as humans.

At the time, these thoughts were just notes. The notes of a young author. But ten years later, it was my turn to suffer a rather foolish accident . . . while dancing. I broke my foot, as well as my coccyx. I was not allowed to even let my foot touch the floor for three months. A broken foot is already enough of a handicap when you try to get around while living in a house or an apartment, but I had had the curious idea to move into a boat with Ziggy that same year. When living on a boat with only one able foot, even the simplest of tasks became problematic, like going to the bathroom, cooking, cleaning, and showering. The boat had only staircases and narrow doorways that certainly didn't accommodate crutches. Even opening cabinets required me to use two hands to undo the safety latch that was in place so the doors didn't swing open while sailing the boat. The only exclusion from my problems was the boat ramp to and from the dock. Moving all my belongings and my cat for three months seemed like an impossible option, so I had to organize things differently.

In those first days, who planted himself in front of me when I tried to extract myself from the couch to go to the bathroom, when I didn't yet know how to take a shower, let alone walk? Ziggy.

Ziggy would blink his eyes slowly and purr at me, as if to say, "It's your turn now to adapt. Find new solutions to live like you used to, do what you need to do, and pick your life back up again." Like him, I needed to reinvent every movement and action in my daily life. I needed to find new tricks, such as ascending the stairs on my knees and descending by sitting down on my side. Like him, instead of running like a feline, I had to hop around like a rabbit.

Like him, I had to learn how to feed myself, to cook differently, to make sure everything was within arm's reach. Like him, I had to adapt each detail of my day, all that I used to think was obvious and easy to do just yesterday. I had to install a new desk, so I could be in a reclined position while I wrote, because I could not hold a sitting position for very long with my broken coccyx.

But across all these small, everyday challenges that demanded what seemed to be a hundred times more effort and time than before, I started to dip my toe into the cat's way of taking his time—the cat's *art de vivre*.

Taking my time to live. Taking my time to perform each motion of the day. I began to immerse myself in the present moment, to feel each minute of life drip away without ever stopping. I began to consciously accept each minute serenely, without feeling like I was losing a single one.

Those three months, under the watchful eye of Ziggy, became my most prolific period of writing in terms of pages and in the number of books I finished. In ten years of writing since, I still have yet to write as much as I did then. I had adapted, but not only to the challenges of taking a shower and getting dressed. I also adapted to writing differently. I wrote more effectively, I was more direct in my words, and I had the courage to dive deeper into the essence of every topic. The truth is, even with my foot and coccyx aside, I was suffering. I wanted to interact differently with people and change my attitude about things. I wanted to be of service to those who might someday end up reading my work.

Throughout these many weeks, Ziggy slept on my piles of folders and heaps of papers at the foot of the couch. I started to rifle through the piles he slept on and uncovered many forgotten, unfinished manuscripts. There were only new discoveries to be made from these ideas I had put aside. I began to see things in a new light and to write with more tenacity—like a cat waiting patiently in front of a mousehole—without letting my mind get distracted by anything, without ever letting my eyes stray from the goal of finishing.

Throughout many years, and especially during those three long months, Ziggy was the soul of every space we shared. He infused each room and each home with his presence.

We understood each other, often without even needing to speak. Sometimes, he guided me with his attitude, with his imperial calm, forcing me to pause and see the bigger picture. I had always been fascinated by his sense of nonattachment, of his comfort in letting go. He was a sage that, even now, I would eventually like to become.

If we are indeed willing to open up, to become sensitive and curious, a cat's presence in our lives can open the door to something impalpable and undefined.

It's complicated to define this sensation in words. But as soon as you are in the company of a cat—a cat you wholly share your life with, a cat who sits next to you watching the sunset, fixed on the fading sun, and who then turns to give you that friendly glance—it's like he has given you access to a world that is more vast, more calm, more grand. You view things from a different point of view and with more soul. You feel more at ease and confident. The little, everyday worries suddenly feel far away, and it's like he has redrawn the order of your priorities. You forget for a moment the big moments from the past and those to come in your life, because at that very moment, the joy of this present moment is the only thought that occupies your spirit.

Ziggy inspired me so much that it was like he could become transparent in my universe, because he was my universe and I was nested inside it. His ambience emanated from every wall, his light and vibration could be felt in every room, whether or not he was actually present there.

We were completely interconnected in a way that I can't clearly define. I sensed—and I can still sense—his presence, like he could sense mine, even from a distance.

I speak of Ziggy in the past tense because today he is already off somewhere, running to find his sister, in a place where the fields and the forests are infinite, where the sunsets are a moment for silent communion between all the beings who have left this earth. I miss him, even though I still sense his presence. He was, even in his last months, the unique witness of my daily life for fifteen years.

The last trace of Ziggy's teachings that he left behind is that—like him—I need to reposition myself in front of every problem, every question, and every obstacle, and observe it from a new point of view to better understand it.

Today, when I find myself faced with a doubt, a problem, or a big decision, I always ask myself, "What would Ziggy do in this situation?" Approach it from the front? Circle it? Take higher ground? Reevaluate the stakes? Act indifferent? Confront it? Negotiate? Be stubborn about it? Dodge it? Hold my ground? What would he do? He would follow his instincts and act only in favor of his well-being and in a way to better his happiness.

Now, when I change my point of view and listen to the little voice inside me, I find that the simplest, fastest, and most efficient solution appears. One that corresponds above all to my happiness, my well-being, and my wishes.

As I write these words, I am thinking of him. It is almost midnight in France, and my two new companions in life, the young Néo and Wallace, are sleeping peacefully next to me.

We can't replace one cat with another. Each and every one—like us—is unique. I hadn't thought to adopt any more cats after Ziggy. I didn't want to relive his departure in the years to come. And yet chance happens upon our path in life, giving us what we need most at that time. I came to realize that when my path crossed with these two bundles of fur, their presence in my universe and throughout my whole life is so vitally important. Here they are always, to show me the way forward. They show me how, through moments, a smile of innocence can wash over my face and how I can remain amazed and curious at the grand show that is this life of ours.

LEFT Brother David

Memories of Cats I Loved

Brother David Steindl-Rast

Clopatra (Cleopatra), 1940s, Vienna, Austria

My family had moved to Vienna, the car had been confiscated, and train rides were a nightmare. It wasn't the worst of the war yet. There was still glass in our windows and only a few small cracks in the walls from the bombs.

On an early, misty winter evening, one of us, I can't remember who it was, heard a soft meow in the john of our apartment; a cat had gotten into the ventilation duct. Well, it didn't take us long to liberate her, give her a good brushing, and find a name for her. Since a john is called *klo* in German, Clopatra (Cleopatra) sounded close enough to the humble place where she had first appeared, yet dignified enough for a cat—and this was no alley cat, to be sure.

We boys couldn't stop marveling at her appearance, and I mean both her sudden coming into sight and her sleek beauty. She was "at least Egyptian," we decided, and fully deserved her name. Her color was beige with an apricot sheen, and at points of special accent—her ears, her paws, her spine—shadows the color of precious wood glided over her short fur as she moved noiselessly. I cannot remember the color of Clopatra's eyes, or rather, every time I try to recall them, I see my mother's eyes instead.

We hardly could believe that Mother allowed us to shelter that cat. We were starving; where would anyone find food for a cat? The couple from whom we bought milk had the surname Spärlich, which in English means "skimpy," and that was an appropriate adjective for a family's weekly allowance of milk. Not much later, the couple was killed by the bomb that destroyed their dairy, but at this time Mother could still go and put a few drops of milk on a saucer for Clopatra. We were speechless, which rarely happened to teenagers, then as now. None of the generous gestures my mother made throughout her life ever impressed me more.

Not only that. My mother put her rose-quartz bracelet around the cat's neck, and its beads seemed to change color until they perfectly matched the hue of the fur. Two days later, this apparition of perfect beauty, at a time when we most needed it, vanished again, but she left the rose-quartz bracelet on Mother's dresser, and in us she left a strange sense of having been graced by a Presence, a feeling stronger than the sadness of missing her.

At the end of the war, plundering soldiers made off with the bracelet. Was it for this that the cat had left her royal collar behind? But even when asking this bitter question, I could still see Clopatra lapping up those precious drops of milk, and in my memory, she had my mother's eyes.

Mietzi, 1980s, New York City

For millennia, humans have speculated why some of us are born into riches, others into rags. If we can't answer this question for humans, how shall we answer it for cats? Bad karma, you say? If so, Mietzi must have misbehaved quite badly in a previous incarnation to be born in a flooded basement this time around. No one knows. What we do know, however, is that the most disadvantaged pull most strongly on our heartstrings, and so someone rescued Mietzi and her siblings from their sunless island of soggy rags. No one ever mentioned the mother cat, and I don't know what happened to the other kittens of that litter. All I know is that little Lisa persuaded her reluctant grandmother, and so Mietzi became my mother's cat.

After that deluged basement, even a tenth-floor New York apartment that was never designed for pets must have appeared like paradise to the poor kitten. Or so we were hoping. Lisa delivered Mietzi in a soft-cushioned basket, and the cat was still sitting in that basket when, after an elaborate farewell from the cat, Lisa kissed her grandmother goodbye at the door. The door closed, Mother turned around, the basket was empty.

That the cat was gone was bad enough, but her pitiful meow was not gone. It kept haunting the apartment for the next hour, while Mother, eventually with the help of her neighbors on both sides, searched every corner so methodically that Scotland Yard would have been proud of that job. The voice, unaccountably, always seemed to come from nowhere; yet it persisted.

When the ladies finally dismantled the Sony radio and hi-fi record player my mother won at a raffle, Mietzi emerged from the only place where she could have gotten as covered with dust as she did: one of the loudspeaker boxes. A bad start, especially since Mother felt that the kitten needed a bath. (There must have been lots of water signs in Mietzi's natal chart.)

No cat could have been more loved, more talked about in telephone conversations with children and grandchildren, more lovingly reported on at length in every letter.

Mietzi wasn't young anymore when Mother was diagnosed with leukemia. Mother was still at home, and I was with her during the decisive days when the doctor was testing whether or not medication could help her. I was sitting by Mother's bed then, when Mietzi seemed to get ready for an acrobatic stunt. Balancing on the back of the rocking chair, she was clearly considering jumping from there onto a high chest of drawers.

Never before had she tried this. Ears laid back, Mietzi was measuring the distance. "Is she going to make it?" I asked—and the moment the words were out, I realized that this was the question my brothers and I were anxiously asking about Mother at that time. "Let's see," Mother replied. Nothing else was said—neither then nor later—but both of us knew what was at stake. There was no tinge of superstition about this. Everything hangs together

> In us she left a strange sense of having been graced by a Presence, a feeling stronger than the sadness of missing her.

with everything; we know that. In principle then, we may look at one event and find in it a clue for quite a different one, unconnected though they may appear to be. Some try this with tea leaves or planets; others think that, in practice, this is too complex an art. There are moments, however, when an omen lights up with such clarity that it would be difficult to deny its foreboding. Not wanting this to be true, Mother and I knew, nevertheless, what was going on here.

Mietzi steadied herself on the back of the rocking chair, crouched, jumped, and missed. Have you ever noticed the embarrassment of a cat when something like this happens? We tried to console Mietzi, Mother and I, but we couldn't quite console ourselves that evening.

The verdict was in. What was not decided was how we would handle it, and that is what really matters.

Mother handled it with grace. Two days later, she was in the hospital again, never to return home to Mietzi. Her mind was clear to the last, as she took care of unfinished business calmly and efficiently. She knew in which folder important papers were kept, in which dresser; she handed my brother the keys with a smile. Only once did she break down and cry: when Mietzi's future was to be decided. But a solution was found: since Mother's apartment was at the same time the office for her charitable work, which my brother would continue, Mietzi could stay where she was. The "super" of the building, who was fond of Mietzi anyway, would look after her when my brother wasn't there. Mother was at peace.

I sat next to her bed holding her hand, and she said, "This is how I'd like to die. You ought to sit there holding my hand and I'd just fall asleep."

"Well," I said, "I'd like that, too, but we can't plan it with such precision." Not many hours later, I was sitting in that very spot holding Mother's hand when she went to sleep for good. So peacefully did she breathe her last that there was no telling exactly when she passed from time into the great Now.

Mietzi outlived her by a year or two, mercifully among her accustomed surroundings: the potted plants on which she nibbled once in a while, the old rugs of which she knew every square inch by their smell, my mother's empty armchair on which she curled up when she got lonely.

Smokey, 1990, New Camaldoli Hermitage, Big Sur, California

"Cats are little people in fur coats," somebody said, and this is true of all cats. Applied to Smokey, however, a statement like this would sound far too condescending. When I dream of her, or even when I think of her with my left brain wide awake, Smokey is not little, not smaller than I; she is my equal, my companion, my colleague, even my teacher. When other cats carry on a conversation with me in my dreams, I'm always a little surprised; with Smokey it would surprise me if she behaved like a mere cat.

When I first saw her, it was her outward beauty that fascinated me. That was at Adam's cottage where Smokey would sit on the fence, a gray shape shifting from one elegant pose to another still more elegant one. There was not a flaw in her evenly silver-gray coat, and the balance of her ever-changing outline was equally flawless. On closer inspection, her fine nose and the twenty balls of her toes were evenly black, her eyes tangerine, and the skin underneath her coat, when one parted her fur by daylight, was sky blue. Only the little rosebud of skin under her tail was pink.

Carthusian monks in France, I later learned, cultivated this breed of cats that Crusaders had brought back from North Africa. Maybe five hundred years of selective breeding caused Carthusian cats to lose their voices, or maybe they were chosen in the first place for being talented mousers who wasted no time talking. In any case, they keep monastic silence better than some monks. Smokey was a master in the use of the silent meow. She'd look up at you with eyes that could pull on anyone's heartstrings and mouth her request inaudibly. When Adam had to be away in the hospital for a long time, he asked me to feed Smokey. I fed her at his place, but she made herself more and more at home in the cell where I lived.

After Adam died, I inherited Smokey—with no contestants to his last will and testament. Smokey herself was old by that time, though no one knew how old. An eccentric lady in Carmel, who had befriended Adam, kept Carthusian cats. I wrote to her, but she was around ninety then and couldn't remember if she ever gave Smokey to Adam.

Gradually, Smokey herself began to show her age. She'd sneeze a great deal, and Dr. Dummit, putting a stethoscope to her chest, said, "Well, I'm no vet, but I can hear all sorts of alarming noises in there." One night, Smokey lay down on a shelf where I'd never seen her lie before and seemed unable to move even her ears. She seemed more than half gone. I blessed her with an image of Saint Martin de Porres, who founded the first animal hospital in the world—in Lima, Peru, in the century after Columbus. Then I put my hands on her back and channeled all the blessings of aliveness into that limp body; I did this for two hours or more. Then I carried the motionless body to Smokey's place at the foot of the bed, slipped under the blanket, and fell asleep.

Several times during the night I woke up; Smokey was still motionless in the same spot. In the morning my first thought was a question: *What will I do with the dead cat?* Hesitating, I opened my eyes. Smokey opened hers at the same time, arched her back, yawned, and jumped with one leap from the bed to the floor. Obviously she had lost only one of her nine lives.

When she lost the ninth one, I happened to be thousands of miles away in the Austrian Alps. A telephone message informed me that she had died on Brother Kieran's lap. He was my neighbor and friend and took care of the cat while I was away. On that afternoon I got only the message. Long afterward, when I returned home, he was reluctant to speak about Smokey's end. That was all right, since I was reluctant to ask. They had buried her in the garden where she had hunted among the lavender bushes and rolled in the crabgrass. Julian sandblasted her name into a hunk of serpentine I had lugged up from Sand Dollar Beach as a grave marker for Smokey.

ABOVE Kelly

LEFT Itsy-Bitsy

Adopted

Kelly McGonigal

In 2005, I was twenty-eight years old, living alone in San Francisco, and looking for a new apartment. I had finished graduate school the year before, and was working as a freelance writer and editor while teaching yoga at studios around the Bay Area. During my hunt, I read a book by the artist SARK, in which she describes stumbling upon a sign in San Francisco in 1989 advertising a magic cottage for rent. As I visited one dismal apartment after another, each more depressing than the last, I lamented, *Where was my magic cottage?* One day, desperate, I wandered the streets of San Francisco, looking at flyers stapled to telephone poles, hoping for a SARK-like miracle. That very evening, when I got home, I found a new post on Craigslist advertising "Magical Cottage for Rent!" I made an appointment and met the landlady the next day, bringing with me my checkbook and credit report.

Behind the cottage was a private garden, complete with a three-foot-tall Laughing Buddha statue. The statue was a bigger version of the very same buddha I had kept in the small garden plot I had tended when I was a graduate student. The landlady assured me that the buddha came with the apartment, despite not knowing which tenant had left it or how long it had been there. It was a sign, I thought. This was my magic cottage. As I signed the lease and wrote a check for the first and last month's rent, a small, short-haired black cat appeared outside the sliding-glass door to the garden. The cat sat at the door and stared at us with yellow-green, slightly crossed eyes. "Who's that?" I asked, surprised and charmed. "Oh, don't worry about that stray cat," the landlady said. "I'm sure if you ignore it, it will go away."

It didn't go away. As I discovered, my garden was the epicenter of a feral cat colony. The person who had lived in the cottage before me had fed the cats on a semiregular basis. A neighbor who had indoor cats would also occasionally leave out a can of food for the feral cats. Although I had moved in with my own indoor rescue cat, I gladly stepped into the role of colony caregiver. I named the regular cats Shadow, Tinkerbell, Mouse Patrol, and Princess.

But it was that very first cat I met at the cottage—the one who stared at me through the glass door with crossed eyes—who I fell in love with. I named him Itsy-Bitsy. He was smaller than the other cats. Skinny, but not starved. He was all black except for a tuft of white fur over his heart. He was the spitting image of the cat in a framed photograph I had bought at IKEA a few months earlier. (Later on, I think there was something magical about that timing—that I had bought the photo so I would recognize Itsy-Bitsy when he appeared.)

Itsy-Bitsy's left ear was clipped, evidence he had been trapped by a rescue organization, neutered, and returned outdoors because he was deemed too wild to be adopted. I should have taken that clipped ear as a sign that Itsy-Bitsy would break my heart. But I fell hard.

Within weeks of my moving in, Itsy-Bitsy would knock at my kitchen window every morning and evening to be petted and fed. He liked to lie outside whatever window I was closest to, moving around the perimeter of the cottage as I moved about. When I went outside, he would run up to have his chin scratched or lie down to have his belly rubbed. He loved to play, and I could make him jump and dance by dragging a stick across the ground. He learned his new name quickly. All I had to do was step outside and call, "Itsy-Bitsy!" and he would come running from whatever hill or nearby yard he had been in. Soon he was waiting for me on the fence outside my front door when I came home after dark. My neighbor would sometimes feed him, thinking he was hungry. But Itsy-Bitsy would stay on the fence until I got home, even if he was fed.

Of course, I wanted to turn this feral cat into a pet, but Itsy-Bitsy was terrified of being in a closed space. Anytime I tried to bring him inside, he ran out. If I closed the door, he howled until he was free again—it was as if I were torturing him. Maybe some traumatic experience being trapped had imprinted this wild response in him. Even outdoors, he had his limits. Although he eagerly presented himself to be petted and rolled on the ground like he was in nirvana as I rubbed his belly, if I tried to pick him up, he became like a fish on a hook. He squirmed and flailed in that way that cats who refuse to be picked up do, until he exploded out of my arms and landed on his feet.

Six months into my stay at the cottage, rainy season came to San Francisco. That year, the jet stream carried storm after storm across the Pacific Ocean from Japan. When it rained, Itsy-Bitsy refused to take shelter. Instead, he sat outside my kitchen window, getting drenched and looking in. I researched online how to build a weather shelter for outdoor cats. My boyfriend, a graduate student living in Seattle, helped me construct a tent out of a blue tarp. We put it outside the kitchen window, under a wooden staircase to the roof of the main house. I hoped Itsy-Bitsy would take refuge in the tent. He wasn't interested. Whenever it rained, Itsy-Bitsy appeared outside my kitchen window, where there was no shelter whatsoever.

> In many aspects of my life, I have been like a feral cat wriggling out of an embrace.

I discovered that if I opened the window and sat on the kitchen floor, Itsy-Bitsy would hop onto the ledge and let me dry him off with a warm towel. He would stay there as long as I did, but if I tried to close the window to keep out the rain, he would panic and bolt. If I left the kitchen floor to do anything else, he would go back into the pouring rain. I spent a lot of time that rainy season on my kitchen floor with the window open. Sometimes I would read a book and drink chai tea while Itsy-Bitsy rested. Sometimes we just sat, and I would pet him, listening to the rain.

One morning Itsy-Bitsy showed up at my kitchen window with a huge, bleeding gash on the side of his head. I cleaned the wound as best I could. He didn't resist. The wound looked too large to have come from another cat's claws. Had Itsy-Bitsy gotten into a scrap with a raccoon or a dog? Had he escaped a hawk or coyote? According to the Society for the Prevention of Cruelty to Animals, the average life span of a feral cat in San Francisco is only five years. I tried again and again to get Itsy-Bitsy to come inside. I wanted to protect him from the rain, the predators, and all the other dangers of being a feral cat. I wanted to rescue him.

I never was able to make Itsy-Bitsy an indoor cat. When my lease expired, I moved back to Palo Alto. I had accepted a full-time teaching position in the psychology department at Stanford University, and the commute to campus from my magical cottage involved three trains and a twenty-minute walk on either end. Sometimes, with train delays, it took three hours each way. I couldn't stay in the cottage, and I couldn't take Itsy-Bitsy with me. Of course I wanted to. But I knew the outdoors was his home.

I arranged to have the woman who lived next door take over feeding Itsy-Bitsy. We practiced before I moved. I made sure Itsy-Bitsy knew where his food would be from now on. I left a bag of dry food with my neighbor and said a tearful goodbye.

A year after I moved out, the woman who took over feeding Itsy-Bitsy emailed me to let me know he was okay. I was so relieved. But she also wrote, "For quite a while, Itsy-Bitsy sat out on the fence by your door waiting for you to come home at night." When I read those words, I cried. I was heartbroken. I took it as proof that I had abandoned Itsy-Bitsy. The image of him waiting for me on the fence felt like evidence that I was the kind of person who let others down.

For a long time, I grieved over my failure to rescue Itsy-Bitsy. I'm almost embarrassed to admit how much shame I felt over not being able to turn him into an indoor cat. I carried it with me for years.

As I was writing this essay, I talked with my husband about my guilt over not being able to protect Itsy-Bitsy. He listened patiently, then said, "You know, I never really thought Itsy-Bitsy needed protecting." He reminded me of the time a raccoon had snuck up behind Itsy-Bitsy while he was eating from his bowl outside my kitchen window. Itsy-Bitsy turned around, hissed once, and returned to his kibble. The raccoon retreated. By all outward appearances, Itsy-Bitsy was the least vulnerable cat in the colony. Not skittish and hypervigilant like Tinkerbell. Not wary and always hiding in the bushes like Shadow. Not slinking around corners, belly close to the ground, like Princess. Itsy-Bitsy was fearless, confident, healthy, and happy.

"Maybe Itsy-Bitsy was protecting you," my husband mused.

I scoffed at this suggestion when he made it. But later, as I thought more about that year in the cottage, his comment rattled around my brain. My whole life, I've found it easier to offer compassion than to receive it. To be the one helping, not the one who needs help. It is hard for me to recognize when someone cares about me. In many aspects of my life, I have been like a feral cat wriggling out of an embrace.

I remembered something Itsy-Bitsy did after I'd been feeding him for a few weeks. In between meals, I left his food bowl outside the kitchen window alongside a bowl of fresh water. One morning I woke up to find a dead mouse in the otherwise empty food bowl. At the time, I thought Itsy-Bitsy was telling me I wasn't feeding him enough. I assumed the mouse was a friendly nudge to keep the bowl full. Later, when I got more involved in animal rescue, I learned that leaving dead rodents can be a form of caregiving. It's unlikely Itsy-Bitsy was scolding me for not providing for him. He might have been worried I wasn't a strong enough hunter to feed myself. It's possible he was sharing his bounty to make sure *I* didn't go hungry. In researching this essay, I read an interview with a cat behaviorist who said that a fresh corpse is how a cat lets you know that you are family. In leaving me the mouse, Itsy-Bitsy might have been saying, "I'm adopting *you*."

If the dead mouse was an act of caregiving, not a complaint, what other behaviors might I have misunderstood? When Itsy-Bitsy waited up for me, sitting on the fence in the dark, was he waiting for dinner—or did he want to make sure I got home safely? When he appeared, on command, anytime I called "Itsy-Bitsy," was he responding to the possibility of food or play? Or did he think *I* needed *him*? Why did Itsy-Bitsy show up at my window every time it rained? I thought I was protecting Itsy-Bitsy. But maybe Itsy-Bitsy was checking on me. Maybe he didn't want to leave until the rain stopped because he was keeping me company.

I know, it's ridiculous to try to read the mind of a feral cat. I don't take any of these interpretations too seriously. But just considering them has broken open something inside of me. My mind reels thinking that I might have been the recipient of a cat's caregiving instinct—that the universe sent me the cottage not because the colony needed a caregiver, but because I needed a cat colony.

Now I look back at that year with wonder. How my "magical" cottage appeared, like magic, on Craigslist the very day I wished for it. How the tiny black cat from my framed IKEA photo appeared, like destiny, at the cottage door. How at a time I was living alone and struggling to find my place in the world, the universe gave me cats who needed to be fed every day. It was a purpose that filled some deep need in my soul. Never in my entire life have I felt as absolutely *necessary* as when I sat on the kitchen floor, in the rain, with Itsy-Bitsy purring. In those moments, I could not doubt that I was exactly where I was supposed to be. I always thought Itsy-Bitsy needed me, but the truth is I needed Itsy-Bitsy. Sixteen years ago, I could only see the year with Itsy-Bitsy one way: I had failed. I was an unworthy guardian. Now I wonder who was guarding whom.

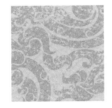

ABOVE   John and Adam, a cat friend in Botswana

Way of the Leopard

John Lockley

Cats seem to embody all the mysteries of the universe in their endless ability to intrigue, mystify, and delight the world around them. They possess an otherworldly quality, which is why no witch is complete without her beloved cat and broomstick, and no Egyptian priestess is complete without her trusted guards of warrior cats holding vigil in her quarters. In mystic circles it is said that if you want to know the state of the universe just look deeply into your cat's eyes and you will enter another dimension—a dimension wholly different from the human world with all our foibles, wants, and needs. To look into a cat's eyes is to look into the eyes of Mother Nature and stand in awe, fear, and uncertainty—for no one can say with confidence what a cat's next steps will be.

I didn't grow up with cats because one of my family members was allergic to them, so we had dogs. However, cats seemed to find a way into my heart and personal space in the most intriguing ways. My cat journey began in the same way as my *sangoma* (traditional African shaman) journey: in the *zendo* (meditation room) of our local Zen center during the early 1990s in South Africa.

This center was frequented by a pair of cats, and one cat in particular was unforgettable. His name was Pudding. He was a huge black cat, weighing the same as a small poodle, with a gnarled-up tail, ear, and an attitude to match. He had more personality than the average human and stalked his way around the meditation center. Pudding helped me meditate! I always knew I had a good sit when he would start pawing me and purring with such delight it sounded like a steam train was around the corner.

Pudding was the bouncer extraordinaire in our little band of meditators, always patrolling the periphery of our meditation center. When he felt someone's "vibe" was right for him, he settled in the lap of the lucky meditator. Occasionally he would show his love and high esteem for us by bringing an assortment of mice and birds. They were mangled, bloody, and injured while he marched them toward us with a slap of his paw and an unemotional turn of the head. We tried to explain to him that as Buddhists we were against all forms of violence and torture. However, he couldn't understand our loud shouts and hoots when all he wanted was to give us animal presents from the larder of nature.

His actions served as a counterpoint to our love-and-light sensibilities. He brought a wild hurricane of natural energies into the heart of our dharma room, making us aware of both the fragility of life and complexities of nature. We loved Pudding! He could be so loving, calm, and gentle. But he could also be a killer of note. And when he was at his stalking best, there wasn't a bird, mouse, or small land creature safe around him. He was an apex predator, surpassed only by ourselves—human beings.

Over the last twenty-six years I have since befriended numerous cats while traveling the world. They would always arrive at a special time. In those moments it felt as if time stopped and the portal to Mother Nature opened to bestow a small teaching. These moments felt uncanny. I had to listen carefully to absorb their impact.

Pudding taught me about cats' ability to teach in a multidimensional way. They move through space and time as if they are on a divine mission, and no matter how much you might want to cuddle and hold them, if it is not on their agenda, forget it. No amount of bribes, cuddles, or soft words will endear you to cats. And when you least expect it, they arrive, ready to offer you everything they have, like a mystic experience at the end of a long exhalation. Time stops, the cat winks, and Mother Nature laughs. Cats embody what I like to call "the mystic pause" or "paws." When they come to you, it is a moment of mindfulness, a gift from the Universe. And all that is required is to give oneself to the experience completely.

I had another auspicious cat experience in the heart of the South Africa wilderness. My traditional sangoma apprenticeship was nearing completion. I had been an apprentice under my master sangoma teacher, MaMngwevu, for almost ten years. My elders and I went into the African bushveld to pray and prepare me for my final initiation ceremony. This involved going to the sea, river, and forest to invoke the spirits of nature to guide and protect me in my sangoma vocation.

I remember it vividly. We started at sunrise, and by the time we entered the forest the temperature had climbed and we were tired. There was a particular tree that we were walking toward when everyone stopped talking, and one of the elder sangoma women touched my arm and gesticulated wildly toward the tree. I saw a flurry of brown movement, leaving the tree transformed and the space around us singing to an ancient tune.

No one can say with confidence what a cat's next steps will be.

Mum Kwempt, my teacher's closest friend and colleague, started talking to me and telling me about the wild native cat that she had just seen lying on the branch of our prayer tree. She said it was waiting for us. It heard us approaching and could have moved away minutes ago. The fact that the cat waited for us to see it was very auspicious. She said it was a sign that the nature spirits were blessing me. The *Izinyanya* (nature spirits or silent hidden ones) wanted to say hello and let me know that they were with me. She said I was very lucky and that my upcoming initiation was being blessed in the most profound way.

The wild cat is very shy and elusive—even more elusive than the leopard in southern Africa. To witness one in the African bushveld is to witness Mother Nature herself. We made offerings to the tree, the wild cat, and the divine presence we had witnessed. For grace had touched us that day, and I will always remember Mum Kwempt's excited voice and quick hand movements tracing the cat as it moved back toward the forest, like a nature spirit manifesting and disappearing.

Years later I was called to Mexico after a series of dreams in South Africa. In the dreams I saw Huichol medicine men, dressed in the traditional way, a hallmark from a distant time. I discussed with my elders about my going to Mexico. They thought it was a good idea, so I decided to go on a pilgrimage to Mexico. A few months later, I found myself in a yoga studio two hours from Mexico City under a pyramid in a rural area. I looked around the yoga room and started preparing the altar for my upcoming ceremony.

In my mind I was thinking about the trip and what was being asked of me. I paused, breathed, and turned around. In walked two white cats, pure white, from the same litter. They were kittens and had this youthful way about them. They approached me with all the joy and exuberance of six-month-old kittens and proceeded to follow me over the course of the entire weekend ceremony.

During their quiet purring moments and skittish, playful romps they whispered to me teachings of innocence, trust, playfulness, and dignity. As I held them in my arms and breathed in their sweetness, I learned to trust more in my dreams and in the mysteries of Nature, to bind us to her like a strong exhalation or a sea breeze that picks up momentum turning into a tidal wave.

The blessing from the wild cat in the South African forest followed me and pervaded my waking consciousness, guiding me in imperceptible ways. I was living in the United Kingdom around 2013 running retreats and trainings. I had just had a terrible breakup with a woman I was in love with. Sadly, our relationship didn't work for a number of reasons, and we parted ways. As with most heartache, I was almost inconsolable. During this time I was invited to teach in Holland and hold ceremonies with a number of other shamans from around the world. My heart was broken and in pieces, and I wondered how to move forward. All I could do was trust in the wind inside of me and continue to sing, pray, and dance.

I led one of my first Way of the Leopard workshops in a tent on a hot summer day. I was joined in ceremony with a lovely medicine man from North America. I had just made my earth altar, a circular bowl with earth in the center surrounded by African fabric. I lifted my arms and encouraged people to push their feet into the ground and shake their spines. I started to channel the teachings of the Leopard and how they teach us to connect to our intuition, our wild selves and nature.

We danced with such abandon that I forgot about my flute near the altar, and I danced on it with a crashing, splintering sound. I stopped, looked at my precious flute now shattered and thought, *new beginnings*. As I said this, a feral cat entered the room. It had markings similar to a leopard's, with black and white spots. It walked directly toward me, moving its tail around my legs and circling the altar. The whole room was speechless. About fifty human beings stood still while this wild cat from the hills and valleys in Holland decided to bless us with its presence.

No one said a word while the cat continued to circle the earth altar, and then, like it entered, it left, and the workshop continued. I saw this as a sign that my work was being blessed by something greater than me, and all I could do was listen to the signs, breathe, and follow my steps, like the cat, one moment at a time.

For me, this is the karma of cats: allowing us to witness grace and reminding us to trust in our instincts. They teach us about spiritual independence as well as interdependence, nobility, and how to be mavericks. They teach us to create our own steps regardless of whether other people have walked in a particular direction or not. Cats don't care about the opinions of others; they walk in time to their own drumbeat as dictated by their instincts, that sharp collection of senses shaping their world and in turn being shaped by the world. If I ever feel lost or dispirited, I just cast my mind to my previous cat experiences and walk outside. There is always a feline friend walking among the urban jungle, reminding me through their presence that all I have to do is listen to my instincts and smell the wind.

ABOVE Nancy

LEFT Nancy and Freddie

Guru Cat

Nancy Windheart

My first meditation teacher was a cat. He was a tough, semiferal cat named Freddie whose body was scarred and torn. He'd lost both ears to a combination of mites and frostbite; his eyelids were ripped; and he came to me infected with FIV, the feline equivalent of HIV.

At the time Freddie came to me, I was on the music faculty of a large arts school tucked away in the pine forests of the Midwest. Our campus was located close to a state park where people would frequently abandon unwanted animals. Many would show up on campus, seeking food from the cafeteria dumpsters and the kindness of humans—especially the young humans who had the habit of dropping bits of their lunches everywhere they walked.

One day, a particular cat caught my attention outside the building where I worked. He was a black tom, with no ears, torn eyes, a scarred face, and a scruffy, dull coat. It was winter and bitterly cold outside. My heart went out to this cat, and I was determined to see if I could help him.

Within a few weeks, the tough-looking black cat was living in my garage. I named him Freddie. I'm a bit embarrassed to admit that he got his name from the infamous Freddie of the horror movie because he was, at that time, a "slasher kitty." I couldn't approach him or touch him without thick gloves to protect my arms and hands.

He bit. He hissed. He spit. He flailed at me with his scimitar-like claws. He was tough and fierce and clear about what he did and did not want and how he did and did not want to live. He was, on the whole, not a very "nice" cat.

And I loved him.

I loved this cat with all of my heart. I knew in the depth of my being—in some wordless, barely conscious way—that we had a deep soul connection, that we were meant to be together. I knew that he was mine, that I was his person, and that there was a journey we had to make together. I could not know at the time how this journey would change my life.

Within a relatively short amount of time, Freddie made what I now understand was a conscious choice: a decision to trust me, to leave his wild outdoor life and become a cat with a human and a home. He settled down and became a lap cat, my dearest, closest friend, and my first true spiritual teacher.

My spiritual path up to that point had been circuitous and without a clear focus or tradition. After I left the fundamentalist Christian church in which I'd been raised, I voraciously read and studied, trying to find a spirituality that made sense to me. As I pursued my career path as a classical pianist, I also studied the Buddhist teachings of Chögyam Trungpa, and the writings of Christian mystics Thomas Merton, Henri Nouwen, and Hildegard of Bingen. I discovered the works of the feminist theologian Mary Daly and learned to use Tarot cards and the I Ching. After that came forays into paganism, Wicca, and practices originating in Native American and shamanic traditions. Each of these areas of study taught me many things, but none of them led me into a consistent experience of spiritual practice.

It was with animals that I found connection, grounding, and a doorway into what most deeply moved me. Through working in animal rescue and advocacy, I rediscovered my childhood ability to hear, feel, and understand my nonhuman friends' thoughts, feelings, and communications.

These experiences awakened what was most alive in me, and I moved deeper and deeper into the animal world and took my first tentative steps toward leaving my career in classical music. As I opened into the world of interspecies telepathic communication, I began to experience profound changes in both my inner and outer worlds. It was at this time of deep inner transformation that Freddie came into my life.

At the time, it was thought that cats with FIV needed to be kept separate from other cats, and so Freddie lived first in my garage, and then in a separate addition in my house. This required that I commit to a regular period of time each evening where we could spend time together. Freddie and I would sit for hours and just hang out, often sitting in a beach chair that I set up in my laundry room. I didn't multitask; I just sat with Freddie.

As we'd sit together each night, Freddie offered me a visceral, embodied experience of dropping deeply into the lake of awareness that was present underneath my constantly running thoughts. Through his example, which included a kind of energetic transmission that I felt with my whole body, I was able to enter into a relaxed and open state of being where there was no me, no cat, no chair. "We" were simply a great pool of vibrant energy, deeply grounded, connected, centered, and resting. Sometimes we'd both sleep, but mostly I'd find myself in a deep place of awareness that had no edges, no boundaries. Often, insight and wisdom would bubble up, and the clutter that was ever present in my mind and life would simply fall away.

He bit. He hissed. He spit. He flailed at me with his scimitar-like claws. . . . And I loved him.

Freddie's telepathic communication with me was clear and precise. If I popped up into thinking, worry, spinning, or obsessive thoughts, he'd wake up, look at me with intense clarity through his torn and scratched eyes, and send me the clear message: "You've left. Come back." And with that guidance, I could. He'd put his head back down and close his eyes, and I'd drop back into presence and awareness. Through his example, I learned that rather than trying to control or remove my frenetic thoughts, I could simply allow them to exist on the surface and drop "beneath" them into an ocean of awareness that was Freddie's natural state.

I discovered that the essence of this quiet, open, deep space of pure presence that I shared with Freddie was love. It was not the confusing, complicated human version of what we often know as "love," but a pure, deep, connected flow of energy, devotion, and presence that I could feel with every cell of my body.

With Freddie's body in my lap, and our shared experience of deep presence and connection, I discovered that love and awareness were not separate things. I was love, he was love, we were love, love was. We floated together in a lake of love. Everything was love—just love.

I didn't realize at the time that this was what people called "meditation." I was simply spending time with my cat, my beloved friend, and sharing an experience that helped me to relate to my life and the world in a different way than I'd known. It was years later, when I learned meditation practices from human teachers, that I realized what Freddie had taught me.

Freddie became my wise, loving lap-cat guru, but he always hissed at me. It became our little inside joke. He would hiss at me, and I would hiss back at him, in my best imitation of semiferal street cat. I would laugh, and he would look satisfied and amused.

Eventually Freddie's FIV brought his body down, and he died in the year of my fortieth birthday. My heart cracked wide open—and as I grieved the loss of his physical presence in my life, I knew that our relationship was alive and would continue in a new form. I continued to feel the essence of his spirit surrounding me, and I knew that he was not gone but had shifted into a different state of being.

Two years after his passing, Freddie came to me in a vision on New Year's Day. He communicated to me, "It's time. This is the year you step onto your path and begin your training as an animal communicator."

I listened to him. I listened to Freddie because I trusted him more than I had trusted anyone in my life. He knew. He knew everything. I began a period of several years of training and apprenticeship, with Freddie's wisdom, guidance, and clarity supporting me each step of the way.

My life changed profoundly and dramatically from that time on, leading me in directions I never could have imagined. I left my job teaching music, began my journey as a professional animal communicator, and now have a life I could never have imagined all those years ago, teaching an international community of students and professionals a curriculum that has its roots in the teachings I received from Freddie.

I now perceive Freddie as a spirit guide, an energy that is much bigger and vaster than could have been contained in his small cat form. I remain in communication and connection with him daily, and he continues to teach me and guide me. He continually reminds me of the true nature of reality, the web of connection that I perceived in my childhood—the fundamental, universal, creative fire of love. Usually his guidance is gentle, clear, and loving, but when necessary, I hear his unmistakable, kick-in-the-pants hiss.

ABOVE Tangy

LEFT Jeff

My Beautiful Tangy

Jeff Foster

held you in my arms as you passed into infinity. Your tangerine-colored eyes, once so enthusiastic and alert, now dulled through so many days of pain, closed for the final time in this incarnation. You were so tired and so ready to rest.

For days you hadn't been able to find comfort; the tumor was pressing against your vital organs. We weren't ready to say goodbye, but when are we ever? Without fear, without panic, without a story, without resistance, you breathed your final breath. I felt your whole body relax in my arms, all tension gone, all suffering melting away. You showed me how to die. You also showed me how to live.

In our back garden, by the grass under the old willow tree, we lowered you into the ground. It was the first time I had seen a dead body. The first time I had lost anyone so close. The first time I had touched the depths of my own grief. You had been such a constant in my life. What happens when our constants vanish?

I'll never forget you, wrapped up in that blanket, so tiny under the willow tree. We returned you to the earth, to the wild. Yet you were never really *ours* to begin with. We gave you a name, but I wonder what your true name really was.

Look at you there, in the turquoise blanket, under the weeping willow, so restful. I have dreamed of you there ever since.

You taught me so much.

You taught me the power and elegance of stillness. You taught me that the destination—the future, the goal—matters so much less than the place where we are today. You taught me how to luxuriate in the present moment, how to live in the senses—in touch and taste and smell and feeling—how to notice everything around me, how to live each day as if there were no other *because there is no other.*

You showed me unconditional love, trust, a dependable presence. However bad I felt, however deep my anxiety and self-loathing became, however piercing my sorrow grew, it was always bearable, and I would survive it. There was something there, something loving, something unshakable, something true, something that would never judge me or reject me or mock me for being the way I was.

There was always *you.* You accepted me exactly as I was. I will never forget the way you accepted me. You mirrored to me my own capacity for self-acceptance. You mirrored Presence. Which I could not find for myself at the time.

You lived in the eternal Now. You lived for the next meal, the next nap, the next chase, for catching butterflies and aggravating squirrels and pigeons. That was your world. Not our human world with its pressures and expectations and "shoulds," a world of adapting yourself to please others. You had no interest in those kinds of games. *You had no image to uphold.* You lived only in the world of the living. The world of mud and sky and rotting leaves, and things to be chased and things to escape, things to play with and things to catch. Our childhood home was your playground and your universe. There was no "outside world" for you; the house and garden were all you knew. And you were happy there, in your little world, which was vast to you, and forever fascinating.

You taught me the essence of true meditation. I must have spent hundreds of hours watching you watching the world. I loved your alertness. Your sensitivity to the tiniest flicker of movement and sound around you. How tuned-in you were to the immediacy of existence. How yesterday and tomorrow were nothing to you—Now was all that mattered. Now was your temple, your canvas, your holy site.

You were completely present, at one, unified with whatever you were doing. When you were sleeping, you slept totally. When you were watching a bird, waiting for the right moment to strike, you were utterly absorbed. When I dangled a piece of string or ribbon in front of you, that was the most important thing in your entire life. You helped me come out of my mind and into the wild—the wildness I had lost touch with. You helped me sink into the clouds and the grass and the trees rustling in the breeze—into the sacredness of a single moment, an unrepeatable moment.

Maybe meditation should be called *sacred purring*.

You taught me fascination. Curiosity. Listening, smelling, tasting, watching, waiting. I loved your patience. Even when waiting, even when doing nothing, you were completely absorbed in the waiting. Even the waiting was fascinating to you. Even the nothing was full of life.

You were never bored. Yes, you had moments of pain and discomfort and struggle and fear. But you were never bored. You were never "switched off." You lived even those moments completely.

I became fascinated with your fascination. I internalized your fascination at a time when I needed that fascination the most. I think you may have saved my life.

You taught without words. You taught without preaching, without superiority, without claiming to have the answers the way some humans do. You taught through silence and through movement. You taught with purrs and growls and meows, with delight at the spring grass and pieces of dust, hamster tails and discarded bits of dinner. You taught with your eyes and your heart and your paws.

You taught me without teaching me. You taught me with your entire being. You were perhaps the greatest teacher I have ever known. Or, at least, the most authentic. You taught simply by being yourself, unapologetically.

* * *

How tiny you were when you first appeared in my life. I was eight years old and was always so afraid I'd find your soft little body with its gray-brown fur under my foot.

You were a little furball of joy. You were a long-haired Persian, a pedigree cat, the daughter of a prize winner. We called you Tangy because your eyes reminded us of the color of tangerines. You had the softest fur—gray and white and black and brown. It was always falling out. Years after you died we still found bits of you all over the house.

Dad didn't want you. But he warmed to you. He ended up falling in love with you. We all did.

You became the one constant in my life, in a life that felt totally groundless and without hope. Most of the time I felt like I was falling. Like I didn't belong in this world and I was meant for another. After long school days of squashing down my feelings and pretending to be something I wasn't, I would throw down my heavy backpack and look for you. I would find you curled up somewhere, lie down next to you, look into your bright-orange eyes. You were always happy to see me.

Sometimes we would talk:

"Tangy?"

"Meow."

"Tangy!"

"Meow."

"Aren't you the sweetest thing?"

"Meow. Meow."

"I love you."

"Meow."

I could have sworn you understood.

I had few friends, terrible social anxiety, and I mostly hated leaving the house. I would spend hours with you in the garden. Sometimes you would curl up at my feet or on my lap. You loved being stroked under the chin. You would let out the loudest purrs. Purrs of pleasure and joy. Purrs that said, *Jeff, we are exactly where we are supposed to be.*

I have never forgotten those purrs. They were so soothing for my frazzled nervous system. At that point in my life, I had no clue how to soothe myself, regulate my own emotions, or even feel them. I felt numb most of the time. I had never known intimacy. I was terrified of it as much as I longed for it. I think you gave me my first taste of unconditional love. Feeling safe with someone. Safe to be authentically myself. The greatest gift of all.

Sometimes, when nobody else was listening, I told you my deepest secrets. You were a generous listener. I shared the parts of myself that nobody else (I feared) would be able to stand. I don't know if you understood. Maybe I was just talking to myself, and that was healing enough. Maybe I just needed a place to vent the unconscious. Maybe I just needed a friend.

Maybe meditation should be called *sacred purring*. Bringing that *purr* energy of friendship into our bodies, soothing our thoughts and feelings with a loving, safe, curious awareness. Purring into the joy but also the pain of life. Purring into the confusion, the doubts, the anger. Purring into the places that ache, the places that feel tense and tight and bound up. Purring into the trauma. Not trying to delete thoughts and feelings, not trying to get rid of them, not even trying to "heal" them at first, but infusing them with a loving purr. Drenching every thought, sensation, every pain and discomfort, every sorrow and anxiety with a warm, curious, kind awareness, a catlike awareness that doesn't judge or reject what it sees but embraces it all as part of the present moment.

And even our nonacceptance, even our frustration, even our feelings of impotence and rage—even they are included.

I sometimes tell people that you were my guru. I'm only half-joking. If you had been in human form, I'd have probably felt the same. Maybe our gurus can come in all shapes and sizes. A cat, a human, a tree. A piece of music. A book. A sacred site. An ordinary place, made holy with our devotion. Maybe you gave me my first taste of true spirituality. A spirituality that includes, that does not divide the sacred from the profane, that sees the extraordinary in the very ordinary.

Many years later, I thought of you as I cared for my father in his final months. The Alzheimer's had seized him, and piece by piece, his world was falling away in that nursing home. In a room of no reference points, no history, no father-son story, we had only the gray walls and whatever came next. I had to be as present with him as you had been with me. The history mattered so much less than the *Being Together*. I loved to sit with him in stillness. To *purr* with him. To be fascinated together with him. To not know the outside world with him but to know this immediacy. And to find fascination even in the boredom. We were cats together, me and Dad. We were exactly where we needed to be.

I sat by Dad's bed in the nursing home as he took his final breath. As he passed into infinity. Back to mother, back to earth, back to rest, his suffering body having served its purpose. I thought of you then. It was the same peaceful death. The same soft presence. The same love, the same light, the same gratitude welling up, the same tears.

Different forms, same infinity.

I, too, will pass into that place one day. I will join you and Dad and all the others. We will be Home together again.

Or perhaps we have always been Home together. Perhaps our true Home lies in the moments we shared. Yes, I think that is where we live in eternity: *in the moments.*

Thank you for the moments. For the meows, the purrs, and, yes, even the scratches. For the human-cat conversations. For the silence.

ABOVE Alice and Surprise

I Was Born to Hold a Cat

Alice Walker

I was born
to hold
a cat.

You may yawn

because
you know
me as
Writer
BIG WIG
This
or
That.

But
I
know
without
any
doubt
that
I was
born
to
hold
a
cat.

I was born to hold a cat.

Her name
was
Phoebe.
We were
complete.
We were perfectly
happy!
Where is she?

I was
seven.
She was
three.
We moved
house.
She
disappeared.

My parents
said,
Well
that
is that.

But I
was
lost
in clouds
of
tears,
for I was
born
to hold
a
cat.

I was born to hold a cat.

There was
no
book,
no
Cat in
the Hat,
in
those
days.

Off I went
into
the world
of books and university
and
trains
and massive
demonstrations,
holding
hands,
singing,
& carrying
signs

that spoke

to our

frustration:

End violence!

Stop the war!

Eradicate poverty

&

segregation!

No child

slavery!

Feed everyone!

House us all

in decent

housing

now!

But in my heart?

Enough

of that.

The question was: Where

is

Phoebe?

Where is

my

cat?

I knew
I was
born
also
for
that: education,
picket
lines,
writing books,
this
&
that.
But
I was
mostly
born
to
hold
a cat.

I was born to hold a cat.

I
married.
I had
children—
in my lap
they
sat.
Loving
them,
still
I
wondered:
Wasn't
I born
to
hold
a
cat?

I thought so: that I was born to hold a cat.

Climbing
Mt. Etna,
crossing
the Seine,
probing
disputes
among
the
refugees
of
the Kingdom
of
Genocidia
&
sharing
bread
with
the
starving
of
Hungaria.
So
much
of
that!

In
my middle
years
I simply
forgot
that
I
was born
to hold
a
cat.

I forgot: that I was born to hold a cat.

In my
heart
a
tiny
door,
kitten size,
sat
tightly
closed.

In my
fine
house
upon
the
hill,
no
messes,
no
rats.

I was happy
or so
I
thought.

But
only
because
I was
asleep
&
never
noticed
the

tiny

door

slightly

ajar,

in my

advancing

age,

behind it . . .

an

empty

space.

Until

one day

from the hedge

there

came

a

sound

while

I was

meditating

quiet

&

still: a meow.

Just

like

that.

And I

remembered, just

like

that,

that

I

was born

to

hold

a

cat.

(*the tiny door inside my heart snapped open wide*)

Out I went

with

a

saucer

of

soymilk

where

the
stranger,
famished,
sat.
Hello, I said,
enchanted by its marbled fur
and
yellow
eyes.
By any chance
are you
my cat?

Fifty years had almost passed. I thought of that. And how I was born to hold a cat.

The stranger
lapped
the
soymilk
then
followed
me
warily
inside
my
house

161

at just

the moment

I saw

behind

the couch

my very

first

rat!

The stranger

napped

before

the

fire.

The house

settled itself

with

a

sigh,

peaceful

&

balanced

at

last,

&

I

began

to

understand.

I named her

Surprise

&

I can

see

holding

her

in

my

grateful

arms

that surprise

itself

is all

of

life

&
this is so
no
matter
what
you do

or do not
do.

Whatever
made
you
feel complete
&
made
you
happy
when you
were seven,
meditate
on
that.

Maybe

you do not

need

to

scale

the

Matterhorn

or

even

ever

see

the

Dalai Lama

in

the

flesh.

Maybe

you

do not

need

to

emulate

Napoleon

in

any

way

or

attend

meetings

where

BIG WIGS

of corporations

define

the

nature

of

global

suffering

for

the

rest

of

the

world.

Maybe

like

me

you can say

I

smell

a

rat!

(*Listen to your hedges*)

I was

not

born

to be

like

that.

I

was born

to

hold

a

cat!

Photo Credits

About the Contributors

Frederic and **Mary Ann Brussat** are the cofounders and codirectors of the Center for Spirituality & Practice and its multifaith website, SpiritualityandPractice.com, which provides resources for spiritual journeys. They are the authors of *Spiritual Literacy: Reading the Sacred in Everyday Life* and *Spiritual Rx: Prescriptions for Living a Meaningful Life*. They and Puja (pictured on top of her cat tree hermitage, page 8) live in Claremont, California.

Suzan Colón is a former senior editor of *O, The Oprah Magazine* and the author of *Yoga Mind: Journey Beyond the Physical*, as well as several other books. A yoga teacher since 2002, Suzan now teaches creative forms of mindfulness and meditation. Suzan has written many profiles on rescue animals and organizations for PetSmart Charities. She and her husband, Nathan, have two rescued Persian cats, Bee and Norman.

Internationally celebrated yoga teacher **Seane Corn** is known for her impassioned activism, unique self-expression, and inspirational style of teaching. She now utilizes her national platform to bring awareness to global humanitarian issues. Since 2007, she has been training leaders of activism through her organization Off the Mat, Into the World, cofounded with yogis Hala Khouri and Suzanne Sterling. Seane has spent time in the United States, India, Cambodia, Haiti, and Africa working with communities in need by teaching yoga, working to stop child labor, and educating people about HIV/AIDS prevention. Seane created the groundbreaking video program *The Yoga of Awakening* and is the author of *Revolution of the Soul*. For more, visit seanecorn.com.

Sterling "TrapKing" Davis is founder of the nonprofit organization TrapKing Humane Cat Solutions in Atlanta, Georgia, which uses Trap, Neuter, Return (TNR) as a focal point to assist, educate, and service communities with feral cat colonies. In the process, he's changing the stereotype that men aren't involved in cat rescue. As TrapKing likes to say, "You don't lose cool points for compassion." Through this work, TrapKing is also bridging the gap in communication between black communities and local animal rescue shelters. There's more information at trapkinghumane.org.

Damien Echols is the author of the *New York Times* bestseller *Life After Death*; coauthor of *Yours for Eternity* with his wife, Lorri Davis; and *High Magick*. The story of his wrongful murder conviction has been the subject of the HBO documentary *Paradise Lost* and *West of Memphis*, a documentary produced by Peter Jackson and Fran Walsh. He and Lorri live in Harlem. Read more at damienechols.com.

Angela Farmer was born in England in 1938 and spent her early childhood during World War II climbing trees, swinging upside down, and helping to care for her three younger brothers. She taught in schools for many years, became an international yoga teacher trained by B. K. S. Iyengar, and traveled extensively in India, inspired by her meetings with remarkable yogis. Now Angela lives with her husband, artist and yoga teacher Victor van Kooten, in a beautiful olive valley near the sea on the Greek island of Lesvos, works with refugees, and teaches her own style of yoga based on listening to the inner body and moving closer to nature. Caring for the local cats, whom she and Victor learn from, are challenged by, and love in so many ways, means life is never dull! Learn more at angela-victor.com.

Jeff Foster shares, from his own awakened experience, a way out of seeking fulfillment in the future and into the acceptance of "all this, here and now." He studied astrophysics at Cambridge University. Following a period of depression and physical illness, he embarked on an intensive spiritual search that came to an end with the discovery that life itself was what he had always been seeking. He is the author of *The Deepest Acceptance*. Visit his website: lifewithoutacentre.com.

The author of *How to Think Like a Cat*, as well as novels, essays, news stories, and humor, **Stéphane Garnier** is also a concept developer, chronicler, and lyricist. His other talents and experience include sound engineer, carpenter, website developer, ergonomic thinker, communications professional, handyman at an oceanographic station, accountant, parcel sorter, hotel manager, database builder, musk salesman, internet R&D specialist, project manager, real estate agent, ashtray emptier, blogger, president of a logo design company, stepfather (yes, it's a profession), poet, microphoto mosaic portraitist, and powerful observer of the human experience. He lives on a boat in Lyon, France, with his cats.

Poet, writer, teacher, and mystic **Andrew Harvey** is a former fellow at All Souls College, Oxford, and has taught at Cornell University, Hobart College, and the California Institute of Integral Studies. He is the author and editor of many books, including *Hidden Journey*, *The Return of the Mother*, *A Journey in Ladakh*, *The Essential Mystics*, *Son of Man*, *The Direct Path*, and his latest book, coauthored with Carolyn Baker, *Savage Grace*.

World-renowned teacher of shamanism **Sandra Ingerman**, MA, is an award-winning author of twelve books, including *Soul Retrieval: Mending the Fragmented Self*, *Medicine for the Earth*, *Walking in Light*, and *The Book of Ceremony: Shamanic Wisdom for Invoking the Sacred into Everyday Life*. She is the presenter of several audio programs produced by Sounds True, and she is the creator of the Transmutation App. Sandra has taught workshops internationally on shamanic journeying, healing, and reversing environmental pollution using spiritual methods. Sandra is recognized for bridging ancient cross-cultural healing methods into our modern culture, addressing the needs of our times. Visit sandraingerman.com and shamanicteachers.com.

Rick Jarow, PhD, is a practicing alternative career counselor, a professor of religion at Vassar College, and author of *Creating the Work You Love*, *In Search of the Sacred*, *Alchemy of Abundance*, and more. His acclaimed seminars, based on years of research and practice with lineage holders in both Eastern and Western traditions, focus on interfacing inner experience with effective action in the world. Learn more at rickjarow.com.

John Lockley is one of the first white men in recent history to become a fully initiated *sangoma* (shaman) in the Xhosa lineage of South Africa. He trained under Zen master Su Bong, and spent ten years in apprenticeship with Mum Ngwevu, a medicine woman from the Xhosa tribe. John is the author of *Leopard Warrior* and splits his time teaching in South Africa, Ireland, Europe, and the United States. For more, visit johnlockley.com.

Dedicated to veganism, animal rights, and exploring the emotional lives of animals, **Jeffrey Moussaieff Masson** is the bestselling author of more than two dozen books, including *The Secret World of Farm Animals*, *The Nine Emotional Lives of Cats*, and *Beasts: What Animals Can Teach Us about the Origins of Good and Evil*. His book *Dogs Never Lie about Love* has sold more than a million copies worldwide. Jeff lives with his family in Auckland, New Zealand. Read more at jeffreymasson.com.

Kelly McGonigal, PhD, is a research psychologist and award-winning lecturer at Stanford University. A leading expert on the mind-body relationship, her work integrates the latest findings of psychology, neuroscience, and medicine with contemplative practices of mindfulness and compassion from the traditions of Buddhism and yoga. She is the author of *The Joy of Movement*, *The Upside of Stress*, *The Willpower Instinct*, and *Yoga for Pain Relief*. Visit kellymcgonigal.com.

Empath **Karla McLaren** is an award-winning author, social science researcher, and pioneering educator whose empathic approach to emotions has taken her through the healing of her own childhood trauma, into a healing career, and now into the study of sociology, anthropology, neurology, cognitive psychology, and education. She is the author of *The Language of Emotions: What Your Feelings Are Trying to Tell You*, the online course *Emotional Flow: Becoming Fluent in the Language of Emotions*, and *The Art of Empathy: A Complete Guide to Life's Most Essential Skill*. Learn more at karlamclaren.com.

Animal communicator, TEDx speaker, educator, and animal parent **Joan Ranquet** is the author of *Energy Healing for Animals* and *Communication with All Life*. She has connected with animals professionally for more than twenty-five years. Joan shares her expertise in animal communication nationally and internationally through workshops, wildlife retreats, and private sessions, and she is the founder of Communication with All Life University, a certification program for animal communicators and energy healers. Joan has been featured in the *Hollywood Reporter*, *Pet Nation*, the *Today* show, *Good Morning America*, *Animal Planet*, and the *Los Angeles Times*. To learn more, visit joanranquet.com.

Theresa Reed has been a professional, full-time Tarot reader for more than twenty-five years. A recognized expert in the field, she's been a keynote presenter at the Readers Studio, the world's biggest Tarot conference, and she coaches Tarot entrepreneurs via numerous online courses and her popular podcasts, *Tarot Bytes* and *Astrology Bytes*. Theresa is the author of *The Tarot Coloring Book* and more than a dozen ebooks and e-courses on Tarot and astrology. She lives in Milwaukee, Wisconsin, and teaches yoga at Inner Divinity Yoga. Read her blog at thetarotlady.com.

Rachel Naomi Remen, MD, is a clinical professor of family and community medicine at University of California, San Francisco, School of Medicine, and the founder and director of the Remen Institute for the Study of Health and Illness at Commonweal. She's an internationally recognized medical educator whose innovative discovery model courses in professionalism and resiliency are taught at more than a hundred medical schools worldwide. Her bestselling books, *Kitchen Table Wisdom* and *My Grandfather's Blessings*, are published in twenty-four languages. Dr. Remen has a sixty-five-year personal history of chronic illness, and her work is a potent blend of the perspectives and wisdom of physician and patient. For more, visit rachelremen.com.

Geneen Roth is the author of ten books, including *This Messy Magnificent Life* and *New York Times* bestsellers *When Food Is Love, Lost and Found,* and *Women Food and God,* as well as *The Craggy Hole in My Heart and the Cat Who Fixed It,* from which her essay here is excerpted. Over the past thirty years, she has worked with thousands of people in her groundbreaking workshops and retreats, and she's appeared on numerous national shows, including *The Oprah Winfrey Show, 20/20,* the *Today* show, *Good Morning America,* and *The View.* Geneen lives in California with charms of hummingbirds; her husband, Matt; and Izzy the fabulous eating-disordered dog, who keeps asking for a kitten.

Writer, teacher, spiritual counselor, and ritualist **Briana Saussy** is dedicated to the restoration and remembering of the Sacred Arts. She studied Eastern and Western classics, philosophy, mathematics, and science at St. John's College and is a student of ancient Greek and Sanskrit. She comes from a diverse lineage of South Texans whose ethnic heritage includes Scotch-Irish, Cherokee, Chickasaw, Mexican, and Jewish roots, which have informed her own experience with fragmented folk magic and storytelling traditions. The author of *Making Magic: Weaving Together the Everyday and the Extraordinary,* Briana lives in San Antonio, Texas, with her husband, two sons, and various furred, finned, and feathered friends. Learn more at brianasaussy.com.

Biet Simkin is a spiritual teacher who fuses more than thirty years of experience with a youthful and rock-and-roll perspective. Raised by an awakened shaman, she pulls out the heart in people through her explosive story, music, and global meditation experiences. Having overcome drug addiction, the death of her father and first daughter (to SIDS), and the burning down of her home, she rose up from the ashes and guides audiences globally to see the world through a new spiritual lens. Featured in *Vogue, Harper's Bazaar, Elle,* and numerous other publications, she has led meditations at the Museum of Modern Art in Manhattan, Sundance Film Festival, and luxury hotels from Los Angeles to the Amalfi Coast. In addition to creating in-room content for 1 Hotel, she has led workshops on how to meditate for executives from Sony to SoulCycle. Her new book *Don't Just Sit There!* teaches us how to live above the laws that prevent us from enlightenment.

Born in Vienna, Austria, **Brother David Steindl-Rast** holds a PhD from the Psychological Institute at the University of Vienna. After twelve years of training in the 1,500-year-old Benedictine monastic tradition, Brother David received permission to practice Zen with Buddhist masters. An international lecturer and author, Brother David is a leader in the monastic renewal movement and in the dialogue between Eastern and Western religions. His most recent book is *May Cause Happiness: A Gratitude Journal.*

Diana Ventimiglia is an editor at Sounds True. For the last fifteen years she's edited everything from romance novels, women's interest books, and personal success stories to inspirational and spiritual growth projects. She's passionate about all things yoga, meditation, rock climbing, and pizza. When she's not editing, you'll find her working through the five-plus books on her nightstand and yelling at her cat, Phillip, to stop knocking things off the shelf. But he's so cute! She lives in Brooklyn, New York.

Alice Walker is an American novelist, short-story writer, poet, and activist. She wrote the critically acclaimed novel *The Color Purple*, for which she won the National Book Award and the Pulitzer Prize for fiction. Her website is alicewalkersgarden.com.

Nancy Windheart is an internationally respected animal communicator and interspecies communication teacher. Her work has been featured in television, radio, magazine, and online media, and she has written for many digital and print publications. Nancy's life's work is to develop deep harmony and understanding between species and on our planet through interspecies communion, connection, and communication, and to facilitate physical, mental, emotional, and spiritual healing and growth for beings of all species through her services, classes, training programs, and retreats. She lives in Santa Fe, New Mexico, with her animal family of dogs, cats, and chickens. To learn more, visit nancywindheart.com.

About Rocky Mountain Feline Rescue

Rocky Mountain Feline Rescue's mission is to care for and shelter homeless cats and kittens until we can find them a permanent, loving home. We are a 501(c)(3) nonprofit organization located in Denver, Colorado. RMFR offers cat-safe indoor and outdoor spaces that allow shelter cats the freedom to explore their surroundings and genuinely interact with people and other cats. We also have a robust foster network of dedicated volunteers who provide healthy environments for RMFR cats. Our cats develop strong social skills, which leads to a high percentage of permanent placements in furever homes. RMFR makes a lifelong commitment to every cat we accept into the shelter, and we prioritize being a safe space for FIV+, FeLV+, and senior cat populations. Learn more by visiting rmfr-colorado.org.

About Sounds True

Sounds True is a multimedia publisher whose mission is to inspire and support personal transformation and spiritual awakening. Founded in 1985 and located in Boulder, Colorado, we work with many of the leading spiritual teachers, thinkers, healers, and visionary artists of our time. We strive with every title to preserve the essential "living wisdom" of the author or artist. It is our goal to create products that not only provide information to a reader or listener, but that also embody the quality of a wisdom transmission.

For those seeking genuine transformation, Sounds True is your trusted partner. At SoundsTrue.com you will find a wealth of free resources to support your journey, including exclusive weekly audio interviews, free downloads, interactive learning tools, and other special savings on all our titles.

To learn more, please visit SoundsTrue.com/freegifts or call us toll-free at 800.333.9185.